ACADEMIC LIBRARIANS AS EMOTIONALLY INTELLIGENT LEADERS

ACADEMIC LIBRARIANS AS EMOTIONALLY INTELLIGENT LEADERS

EDITED BY PETER HERNON, JOAN GIESECKE, AND CAMILA A. ALIRE

LIBRARIES

U N L I M I T E D

A Member of the Greenwood Publishing Group

WESTPORT, CONNECTICUT • LONDON

Library of Congress Cataloging-in-Publication Data

Academic librarians as emotionally intelligent leaders / edited by Peter Hernon, Joan Giesecke, and Camila A. Alire.
    p. cm.
  Includes bibliographical references and index.
  ISBN-13: 978–1–59158–513–8 (alk. paper)
  1. Academic librarians—Psychology. 2. Emotional intelligence. 3. Leadership.
4. Academic libraries—Administration. I. Hernon, Peter. II. Giesecke, Joan.
III. Alire, Camila A.
  Z682.4.C63A335 2007
  027.7092—dc22   2007030133

British Library Cataloguing in Publication Data is available.

Library of Congress Catalog Card Number: 2007030133
ISBN: 978–1–59158–513–8

First published in 2007

Libraries Unlimited, 88 Post Road West, Westport, CT 06881
A Member of the Greenwood Publishing Group, Inc.
www.lu.com

Printed in the United States of America

The paper used in this book complies with the
Permanent Paper Standard issued by the National
Information Standards Organization (Z39.48–1984).

10 9 8 7 6 5 4 3 2 1

CONTENTS

ILLUSTRATIONS

PREFACE

Leadership, which has been defined variously, involves factors such as motivating and inspiring people to create and carry out a shared vision to guide future actions of the organization. Furthermore, leadership is about giving people confidence to meet organizational expectations and serve as change agents. It also encourages them to seek, be given, and benefit from team coaching and mentoring aimed at enhancing their knowledge, skills, abilities, and effectiveness. The staff become both followers and leaders, and they collaborate with other institutional partners.

With so many academic libraries organized into teams or small groups and involved in managing change; with new staff members expected to work together to plan, implement, administer, and evaluate services; and with librarians having to forge partnerships at the national and other levels, librarians are becoming increasingly interested in leadership theories, styles, traits, roles, and development. A thorough understanding of leadership has value to everyone working in people-centered organizations, from staff who are empowered to solve problems that library customers encounter as they seek information, to members of teams and small groups trying to improve the delivery of service to the communities that libraries serve, and to middle and senior managers pursuing organizational effectiveness while intent on changing organizational cultures and engaged in succession management or planning.

An increasing number of job advertisements for academic and public library directorships mention leadership as one of the requirements for a successful candidate. If academic libraries are learning organizations which are undergoing massive transformation, they need leaders who can help their staff develop and accept new educational roles, take advantage of new opportunities, and participate effectively throughout the institution and with assorted stakeholders.

One perspective on leadership, which is the focus of this book, is currently receiving much attention. That perspective, known as emotional intelligence (EI), is linked to effective performance, and it involves managing the mood of the organization. EI contributes to a person's ability to manage his or her own emotions, to monitor the emotional state of others in the organization, and to influence the thinking and behavior of others to accomplish a shared mission or vision.

Academic Librarians as Emotionally Intelligent Leaders complements *Making a Difference: Leadership and Academic Libraries,* which provides an overview of various leadership theories, styles, and issues, and which incorporates the perspectives of a number of academic library leaders.[1] The present book focuses on EI, but does contrast it to other leadership theories, showing that EI is important but not the sole theory of interest to academic librarians.

The topics covered in *Academic Librarians as Emotionally Intelligent Leaders* should be of interest to everyone wanting to understand leadership and to develop the leadership abilities of academic librarians as well as librarians in other work environments. Other audiences include instructors of leadership institutes, librarians leading professional associations, and faculty teaching leadership courses in schools of library and information science. The goal for any managerial leader working in academic or other types of libraries today should be to have a realistic understanding of one's emotions and the emotions of others, as well as to discover effective ways to advance the organization's mission. Librarianship presents both challenges and opportunities. Such a situation calls for effective leadership. EI helps to frame the issues related to how the profession achieves such leadership.

Peter Hernon
June 2007

NOTE

1. Peter Hernon and Nancy Rossiter, eds. *Making a Difference: Leadership and Academic Libraries* (Westport, CT: Libraries Unlimited, 2007).

1

EMOTIONAL INTELLIGENCE

Joan Giesecke

"Leaders have always played a primordial emotional role."[1]

Do you want a new leadership fad? Are you concerned that you are not keeping up with the latest trends? If you answer both questions in the affirmative, join those leaders and managers who are trying to determine if emotional intelligence is real or just a new way to sell books. Is paying attention to emotions more than just remembering to be polite and nice? To answer these questions it helps to go beyond the popular trade books and look at the research in the field. While this is still a new area for research, data have been developed that show there is substance to the theory that emotional intelligence is one of the intelligences that impact how people relate to each other.

To dissect the concept, one can begin by understanding how intelligence is identified. John D. Mayer and Peter Salovey note that, in order to identify an intelligence, psychologists "define it; develop a means to measure it; document its partial or complete independence from known intelligences; and demonstrate that it predicts some real-world criteria."[2]

One challenge in looking at emotional intelligence is to define the term in a way that distinguishes it from other aspects of cognition, motivation, or affect. Some definitions of emotional intelligence do not meet this criterion. For example, Mayer and Salovey remark that definitions that tie emotional intelligence to self-control, persistence, and self-motivation are really concentrating on motivational characteristics rather than on emotional characteristics.[3] These authors prefer the definition that emotional intelligence is "the ability to perceive emotions, to access and generate emotions so as to assist thought, to understand emotions so as to promote emotional and intellectual growth."[4] The definition they use includes the key characteristic of an intelligence, which is that emotional intelligence increases ones abilities.

Other researchers in identifying emotional intelligence distinguish emotional intelligence from traits and talents. Traits are characteristics, habits, or a set of properties a person possesses, and talents are abilities. In leadership theory the traits of intelligence, self-confidence, determination, integrity, and sociability appear to be some of the most important traits for success.[5] Mayer and Salovey distinguish emotional intelligence from such traits by noting that being able to figure out one's emotions is a mental skill while being sociable (i.e., sociability) is a preferred way of behaving or a trait.[6]

Many variations on the definition of emotional intelligence exist in the literature as noted in chapter 2. Nonetheless, the definitions tend to include one or more of the following components: "(a) ability to understand and express oneself; (b) the ability to understand others and relate to them; (c) the ability to manage and control emotions; (d) the ability to manage change, adapt, and solve problems of a personal and interpersonal nature; and (e) the ability to generate positive mood and to be self-motivated."[7] In these components are the two core ideas of emotional intelligence: the ability to manage one's own emotions and the ability to understand and recognize the emotions of others.

EMOTION DEFINED

Before continuing in the overview of emotional intelligence, it may be useful to take a slight detour and look at the word emotion. While the precise definition of emotion may be debated by psychologists, Daniel Goleman uses the term to refer to "a feeling and its distinctive thoughts, psychological and biological states, and range of propensities to act."[8] He notes that the main categories or families of emotions are: anger, sadness, fear, enjoyments, love, surprise, disgust, and shame.[9] These core families are the key components to consider when examining emotional intelligence and form the frame for further analysis.

SKEPTICS

The concept of emotional intelligence is not accepted by all theorists. For example, Lynn Waterhouse argues that there is little evidence to support the concept of emotional intelligence. She notes that many definitions of emotional intelligence and different models have been developed. Therefore, for her, this is evidence that emotional intelligence has not developed to the point where it can be considered a valid theory. Further, she feels that there is a lack of empirical evidence to support the theory. She also questions statements that have been made claiming that emotional intelligence can be used to predict success and is a more predictive measure of success than a person's intelligence quotient (IQ). She cites studies that conclude that emotional intelligence competencies did not predict job success any better than cognitive skills or personality traits.[10]

In response to Waterhouse, Cary Cherniss, Melissa Extein, Daniel Goleman, and Roger Weissberg note that Waterhouse combines scientific claims and popular claims without distinguishing the science from popular literature.[11] These authors agree that emotional intelligence is a young theory, still developing, and still being tested. It is a theory in progress. They note that a consensus on definitions and models is unlikely in the early stages of theoretical work. They also note that there are several models that are being tested that do distinguish between emotional intelligence and IQ, and personality constructs. The authors cite research that links emotional intelligence to success in the workplace and clarify the misimpression noted in the popular literature that emotional intelligence accounts for 80 percent of one's success. Goleman writes that IQ does not predict success among a pool of equally talented top performers. He says that emotional intelligence abilities will better discriminate among a group of people who are all technically capable of competing for a top position.[12]

While the debate about the importance and impact of emotional intelligence will continue, the evidence that emotional intelligence is a set of abilities that can be learned and that can lead to success in the workplace continues to build.

EMOTIONAL INTELLIGENCE

Emotional intelligence models vary slightly on the components that define the model. In *The EQ Difference*, Adele Lynn uses five components to characterize emotional intelligence: self-awareness, empathy, social expertness, personal influence, and mastery of purpose and vision.[13] These elements describe how people relate to their internal and external worlds and the competencies needed to use emotional intelligence effectively.

Academic intelligence and emotional intelligence are not in conflict, but are both important. Academic intelligence is one's ability to handle the knowledge, as well as the intellectual and technical skills needed to perform at a level of excellence. Emotional intelligence provides a person with the skills needed to manage emotions and moods. Emotions can easily overwhelm us or highjack how we are feeling. However, we can learn to recognize when we are feeling swept away and can determine how long that feeling lasts. Emotions that are out of control or that are negative can overwhelm our concentration and make it difficult to focus on the task at hand. Even fairly mundane tasks such as remembering a telephone number can become impossible when the working memory is overcome by emotional distress. Contrarily, positive emotions can enhance our ability to perform the tasks at hand. Positive emotions help improve confidence and motivation so that one can pursue excellence.

Good moods and positive emotions improve flexibility and our success at solving both intellectual and interpersonal problems.

Emotions such as hope and optimism can be great motivators. With hope, one is less likely to give in to anxiety or depression. With optimism, one proceeds expecting success and, if things go wrong, will look for alternatives to achieve success rather than giving up. The self-motivating emotions of hope and optimism aid academic success by helping one to keep going, and to keep trying even when things become frustrating. Positive emotions help us bounce back when things go awry. People unable to summon positive emotions may become depressed, or be unable to dispel a bad mood or stop worrying.

For Goleman then, emotional intelligence is a master aptitude. It impacts all other abilities and can facilitate or interfere with these abilities. "To the degree that our emotions get in the way of or enhance our ability to think and plan, to pursue training for a distant goal . . . they define the limits of our capacity to use our innate mental abilities."[14]

EMOTIONS IN THE WORKPLACE

Studies in the 1970s found that executives felt emotions did not belong in the workplace and that empathizing with employees would make it difficult to make the hard decisions that are part of the organizational environment.[15] Today, while some managers may still feel that the head is more important than the heart and that emotions are not the purview of managers, the research increasingly shows that emotional intelligence does impact organizational performance.

Research studies demonstrate that there is a link between emotional intelligence and work performance, although not as strong as stated in popular texts that still claim that emotional intelligence accounts for or determines 80 percent of a person's success. In their compilation of research studies, Vanessa Unch Druskat, Fabio Sala, and Gerald Mount show how emotional intelligence has been measured and linked to performance.[16] A study of air force recruiters showed that those with higher emotional intelligence scores were more successful than their colleagues. The results showed that factors such as geographic region, ethnicity, gender, or age were not predictors of success. Other studies of the military found that soldiers selected for elite combat units, soldiers nominated for officer training by their peers, and those who expressed interest in office training were found to have higher emotional intelligence scores than their counterparts.[17]

A study of navy alcohol-treatment counselors found that counselors with higher empathy and emotional self-awareness scores were more effective than the average counselor. Training and development programs to enhance these competencies could result in more counselors who are sensitive to themselves and sensitive to others.[18]

A study of executives in the petroleum industry examined competencies that predicted success in this international industry where technical skills are essential. The study found that emotional competencies of achievement orientation, impact and influence, self-confidence, teamwork and cooperation, organizational awareness, empathy, and international flexibility differentiated superior performance from average performance. The three cognitive skills of analytical thinking, conceptual thinking, and information seeking were also key competencies. This research also showed that cognitive and emotional skills were critical to success.[19]

Druskat, Sala, and Mount also include four studies on emotional intelligence and work groups or team success. The studies looked at different competencies and all found that higher emotional intelligence scores correlated to higher team performance. The research also showed that organizational emphasis on external connections over individual aims can lead to higher performance.[20]

DEVELOPING EMOTIONAL INTELLIGENCE IN THE ORGANIZATION

Goleman included questions of managing organizations in his work *Emotional Intelligence*.[21] One area where emotional intelligence comes into play in the organization is in providing feedback to employees. Too often critiques come across as personal attacks and employees play out the same scenarios they use in their families at the workplace. The scenarios become dysfunctional when applied to the workplace. Sarcasms, angry voices, and blanket criticisms only serve to destroy motivation. Employees feel they are being treated as children and may act out in ways that are not productive. Instead, Goleman suggests, as do most management texts, that positive coaching includes concentrating on behaviors and not the person, offering solutions, and being empathetic while discussing difficult issues with employees. For the employee receiving criticism, the challenge is to see the criticism as information that can be used to improve performance. Individuals with high emotional intelligence scores are better able to place the criticism in context and not see it as a personal attack, regardless of how the conversation is approached by the supervisor.

While the research studies cited above provide research evidence of the effectiveness of emotional intelligence, developing emotional intelligence abilities is covered more in popular texts than in research texts. Popular self-help works abound that describe how individuals can become more self-aware, better able to control their own emotions, and better able to understand and influence the emotions of others.

Practical advice for improving one's emotional intelligence is found in texts such as *The EQ Difference*. Here Lynn describes how to develop your own "self-coach" or inner voice to help master emotional intelligence. Lynn's seven steps for emotional intelligence are: observe, interpret, pause, direct, reflect, celebrate, and repeat.[22]

Observing involves learning to be more aware of how one is feeling and how others are reacting. It also involves learning to understand your inner voice and learning to not respond to negative voices. Lynn describes 34 inner voices that can control our actions, from the victim voice, "It's not my fault," to the rabbit voice, "Run for safety," to the critical voice, "It's never good enough." More positive voices include the hope voice, "Tomorrow will be better," the optimist voice, "It can be done,"and the creative voice, "Imagine everything." The positive voices help you maintain momentum and move forward. The negative voices derail you and can cause you to fail. Understanding your inner voices is the beginning of emotional self-awareness.

Interpreting the observations becomes the next challenge. Data need to be organized in a usable way. That is, you need to learn how you generally handle a particular emotion and when you are most likely to act negatively. You also need to know how your reaction impacts others. As you pay attention to your emotional reactions, you build an internal database of your approach to emotional encounters. You can then draw on this database of knowledge to prevent yourself from reacting in a negative or inappropriate way to an emotionally charged situation.

After you have interpreted the data take a deep breath and pause; it is time to count to ten, take a cleansing breath, or do whatever you need to do so you can assess the situation and pick a positive rather than a negative response. Perhaps one of the hardest skills for leaders to learn is to pause and not react immediately to a work situation or problem. Yet, taking a moment to step back will give you a chance to change your predictable but negative response to a more positive response.

The big challenge is directing a change in your own responses. Here is where you need to implement control and change a possible negative response to a more positive approach. Emotional intelligence centers on managing emotions, and that includes managing your actions as you experience your feelings. Managing emotions is not the same as feeling no emotions. Not experiencing emotions is as dangerous as experiencing negative emotions. Lack of feelings leaves one unable to relate to others, to provide leadership, or to engage in the organization. Instead healthy emotional responses include understanding and feeling emotions, and controlling your response.

Reflection is the next critical component.[23] Just as assessment and evaluation are keys to successful business processes, reflection is crucial to learning to change our own behaviors. Through reflection you can assess your responses and move closer to living your intentions. You become more intentional in how you live and how you react to those around you. Reflection is a key part of learning from your experiences.

Next, celebrate successes. Good leaders know the importance of celebrating successes at work. They understand the importance of acknowledging and celebrating goal achievement and employee successes. Yet, too often we forget to celebrate intangible achievements and positive changes in our own behavior. A celebration can help reinforce the importance of making changes in behavior that can lead to success in our lives.

Finally, repeat successes. It is important to find your own ways of improving your emotional intelligence and taking control of your reactions. You choose how you want to react to a situation. Pick a positive approach and you will be more likely to succeed.

The self-coaching approach aims at long-term changes in our behavior to become more aware of the impact our emotions have on our actions. Other authors provide simpler systems and advice to get one started on controlling emotions while building the kind of in-depth database of reactions advocated by Goleman. In a brief article by Dawn Raffel in the popular magazine *O, The Oprah Magazine*, Ana Maravelas, a corporate consultant, suggests that the two self-defeating habits of smart people are to blame others or to blame themselves when things go wrong. Each of these self-defeating inner voices results in frustration and can lead to rage. Instead of giving in to these two inner voices and the resulting emotion or response, Maravelas suggests thinking of these reactions as "stinky twins of BO (blame others) and BS (blame self)."[24] To combat these reactions, she suggests practicing curiosity. Rather than giving in to these destructive emotions, you can start by asking questions, finding out more about the situation, and clarifying your assumptions. By asking questions and keeping a dialogue going, you will move past the initial reaction to a more thoughtful, emotional response.

INFLUENCING THE EMOTIONS OF OTHERS

The second part of emotional intelligence is understanding and influencing the emotions of others. Emotions can be spread among people. One can be influenced by someone else's bad mood. Employees act differently when they believe the boss is in a good mood rather than a bad mood. A bad mood or toxic reaction by a leader can cause anxiety in others, or can cause a group to mirror the leader's behavior, thereby reinforcing a toxic environment. Understanding why these reactions occur and how to manage them is a key part of effective leadership and is the core competency in social intelligence.

Karl Albrecht defines social intelligence as "the ability to get along with others and to get them to cooperate with you."[25] He enumerates the externally oriented competencies that lead to successful interactions with others. Albrecht lists five competency areas that lead to nourishing rather than toxic behaviors: situational awareness, presence, authenticity, clarity, and empathy.[26]

Situational awareness involves observing social interactions and understanding people's intentions. People who can read a social situation and react appropriately are more likely to have positive interactions than those who misunderstand the context and environment in which they operate.

Presence is the effect one has on others. It includes the physical impression one makes as well as the impact that one's mood and demeanor have on others.[27] Presence also encompasses the nonverbal cues one gives off in conversations with others.

Authentic people are those who are honest about whom they are and act accordingly. Authentic leaders are true to themselves while understanding how to manage the perception others have of them. They know which personality traits to reveal and when so that they create a positive impression with others. "Authentic leaders demonstrate a passion for their purpose, practice their values consistently, and lead with their hearts as well as their heads."[28]

Authenticity is not a process of manipulating others. It is a process of understanding how others are reacting and feeling, and choosing to use those parts of one's personality and emotional and social intelligence to influence the behavior of others. Authentic leaders match their words with their actions. They know themselves. They get to know the people with whom they regularly interact. They understand the organizational context in which they operate. Authentic leaders balance these three elements and create an effective environment.

Clarity as a competency is the ability to be clear in communicating both verbally and with non-verbal cues. Clarity in communication involves avoiding jargon, using active voice, and crafting well-structured sentences. Social intelligence, though, includes more than just good communication skills. It also involves using language to advance a discussion rather than to cut off ideas, discourage others, or assign blame. Positive language promotes discussion and encourages others to participate in the interaction.

Empathy is another key competency in social intelligence. Empathy is moving beyond understanding the feelings of others to "a state of positive feelings between two people, commonly referred to as a condition of rapport."[29] By practicing empathy, one establishes a bond with others that leads to positive interactions and improved interpersonal relations.

Leaders who practice these competencies create organizations that have a positive environment. A positive working environment encourages nurturing behaviors rather than toxic behaviors. People are treated with respect and are engaged in the organizations. Further, leaders who practice good social intelligence skills create organizations that inspire employee loyalty and productivity. Leaders who create toxic environments and do not practice social intelligence competencies create organizations with high turnover rates, and with employees who do enough to get by but are unlikely to excel.

CONCLUSION

Emotional intelligence, as backed by the research on this important aspect of ourselves, helps leaders move beyond basic "people skills" to understanding how one's own reactions and feelings impact how one is perceived by others. Leaders and managers need to understand their own emotions and recognize and understand the feelings of those around them. Leaders are more successful when they pay attention to their social interactions with others in the workplace and the impact they as leaders have on those around them. It is also important for leaders to understand the impact that others' emotions have on them. When leaders are aware of the emotional side of the workplace along with the technical processes of getting tasks and goals accomplished, they are better able to create a working environment that encourages excellence.

"Managing your emotions means something quite different from stifling them. It means understanding them and then using that understanding to turn situations to our benefit."[30]

NOTES

1. Daniel Goleman, Richard Boyatzis, and Annie McKee, *Primal Leadership: Realizing the Power of Emotional Intelligence* (Boston, MA: Harvard Business School Press, 2002), 5.

2. John D. Mayer and Peter Salovey, "What Is Emotional Intelligence," in *Emotional Development and Emotional Intelligence: Educational Implications,* ed. Peter Salovey and David J. Sluyter (New York: Basic Books, 1997), 5.

3. Ibid.

4. Ibid.

5. Peter Northouse, *Leadership, Theory, and Practice* (Thousand Oaks, CA: Sage Publications, 2004), 33.

6. Mayer and Salovey, "What is Emotional Intelligence," 8.

7. Vanessa Unch Druskat, Fabio Sala, and Gerald Mount, eds., *Linking Emotional Intelligence and Performance at Work: Current Research Evidence with Individuals and Groups* (Mahwah, NJ: Lawrence Erlbaum Associates, 2006), 4.

8. Daniel Goleman, *Emotional Intelligence* (New York: Bantam Books, 1995), 289.

9. Ibid., 289–90.

10. Lynn Waterhouse, "Multiple Intelligences, the Mozart Effect, and Emotional Intelligence: A Critical Review," *Educational Psychologist* 41, no. 4 (Fall 2006): 216–218.

11. Cary Cherniss and others, "Emotional Intelligence: What Does the Research Really Indicate," *Educational Psychologist* 41, no. 4 (Fall 2006): 239–46.

12. Goleman, *Emotional Intelligence.*

13. Adele B. Lynn, *The EQ Difference: A Powerful Plan for Putting Emotional Intelligence to Work* (New York: AMACOM, 2005), 39–40.

14. Daniel Goleman, *Emotional Intelligence*, 80.

15. Ibid., 149.

16. Druskat, Sala, and Mount, *Linking Emotional Intelligence and Performance at Work.*

17. Ibid., 3–20.

18. Ibid., 81–96.

19. Ibid., 97–124.

20. Ibid., 145–244.

21. Goleman, *Emotional Intelligence.*

22. Lynn, *The EQ Difference,* 48–49.

23. Ibid., 150.

24. Dawn Raffel, "The Two Self-Defeating Habits of Otherwise Brilliant People," *O, the Oprah Magazine* 7, no. 9 (September 2006), 295–6.

25. Karl Albrecht, *Social Intelligence: The New Science of Success* (San Francisco: Jossey-Bass, 2006), 3.

26. Ibid., 29.

27. Ibid., 69.

28. Bill George and others, "Discovering Your Authentic Leadership," *Harvard Business Review* 85, no. 2 (February 2007): 130.

29. Albrecht, *Social Intelligence,* 138.

30. Hendrie Weisinger, *Emotional Intelligence at Work: The Untapped Edge for Success* (San Francisco: Jossey-Bass Publishers, 1998), 27.

2

REVIEW OF RELEVANT LITERATURE

Peter Hernon

"Emotional intelligence is the sine qua non of leadership."[1]

Leaders should not only excel through their abilities, skills, and intelligence, but they should also handle themselves and their relationships with others to achieve a common vision or goal. "The ability, capacity, or skill to perceive, assess, and manage the emotions of one's self and of others"[2] (including groups) is known as emotional intelligence. In their seminal paper, published in 1990, Peter Salovey and John D. Mayer defined the concept as a type of intelligence, more precisely as "the subset of social intelligence that involves the ability to monitor one's own and others' feelings and emotions, to discriminate among them, and to use this information to guide one's thinking and actions."[3] They revised their definition to eliminate vagueness and insert the idea of feelings:

Emotional intelligence involves the ability to perceive accurately, appraise, and express emotion; the ability to access and/or generate feelings when they facilitate thought; the ability to understand emotion and emotional knowledge; and the ability to regulate emotions to provide emotional and intellectual growth.[4]

Emotionally intelligent individuals regulate their display of emotions, and they are cognizant of how they fit in (and contribute) as members of an organization. They communicate effectively with others in the pursuit of organizational goals. They influence how subordinates perceive them and develop effective leader-member relationships. By managing conflict and encouraging supportive member interactions, they create a supportive, nurturing environment.

Antecedents of the concept of emotional intelligence can be traced back to the 1920s and research on social intelligence conducted by Edward L. Thorndike at Columbia University as well as Howard Gardner's 1993 work on multiple intelligence.[5] Although Wayne L. Payne used the term *emotional intelligence* in his 1985 dissertation,[6] it was Daniel Goleman who popularized it.[7] Research directly on the concept originated with Salovey and Mayer starting in the late 1980s—or perhaps earlier with the research of David McClelland on achievement motivation.[8]

Victor Dulewicz and Malcolm Higgs show that the literature on leadership does not confine the interjection of emotions into leadership to a single term, but rather that EI has companion concepts, including emotional competency, emotional literacy, emotional quotient, interpersonal intelligence, and personal intelligences.[9] Mayer and Salovey distinguish between emotional intelligence and emotional knowledge, preferring to use the latter term.[10] This distinction, however, is not widely accepted even though emotions cannot be characterized as a standard type of intelligence (e.g., intelligence quotient). Despite the various terms used, much of the literature still uses emotional intelligence, with the proponents of EI emphasizing its value in the workplace, both for leaders and followers, including members of teams.

TWO MODELS

Two distinct, but related, models of EI have emerged. The abilities model, which Mayer and Salovey support, deals with those "abilities that involve perceiving and reasoning abstractly with information that emerges from feelings."[11] This model connects emotion and intelligence. The competencies associated with the model cluster into four dimensions:

1. appraisal and expression of emotion in oneself
2. appraisal and recognition of emotion in others
3. regulation of emotion in oneself
4. use of emotion to facilitate performance[12]

The mixed model, which Goldman and Reuven Bar-On present, views emotional intelligence as linked to social intelligence and as "an ability with social behaviors, traits and competencies."[13] Those competences, discussed below, include such elements as assertiveness, empathy, self-motivation, and stress tolerance.

Not all of the research examines either model. Still, each model has its proponents, and, so far, there is no evidence that one is superior to the other. This book, however, focuses on the mixed model and the work of Goleman.

KEY WRITINGS OF DANIEL GOLEMAN

In *Emotional Intelligence,* Goleman defines EI as "the capacity for recognizing our own feelings and those of others, for motivating ourselves, and for managing emotions well in ourselves and in our relationships."[14] He argues that the traditional view of intelligence is too limited, and he describes instances in which people with modest intelligence quotients (IQs) succeed while those with higher IQs do not. He attributes this success to an ability to understand and manage emotions. This ability, known as emotional intelligence, focuses on *knowing yourself, managing yourself, recognizing others' emotions,* and *managing others' emotions.* Incidentally, there is only one indexed reference to the word *leadership* in the index.[15]

In *Working with Emotional Intelligence,* Goleman asserts that emotional intelligence is the most important factor in the success of a leader; conversely a leader's lack of emotional regulation is related to leader ineffectiveness. Furthermore, emotional intelligence accounts for more than technical intelligence in determining whether individuals in leadership positions become rising stars or simply achieve mediocre results in the workplace. Emotional intelligence, he explains, consists of a learned set of competencies that determine how leaders interact with people. These competencies fall into two broad categories: personal and social competencies. The former includes self-awareness, self-regulation, and motivation. Social competencies, on the other hand, include empathy and social skills, and the relevant sub-competencies.[16] Each of the categories contains sub-competencies.

In "What Makes a Leader?" which appeared in the *Harvard Business Review,* Goleman refers to personal competencies as relating to self-management and social competencies as relating to managing relationships. He summarizes the five categories, now called domains: self-awareness, self-regulation, motivation, empathy, and social skill.[17] He concludes that leaders "need to have" the components of emotional intelligence to be successful leaders.[18]

In *Primal Leadership,* Goleman, Richard Boyatzis, and Annie McKee state,

Understanding the powerful role of emotions in the workplace sets the best leaders apart from the rest—not just in tangibles such as better business results and the retention of talent, but also in the all-important intangibles, such as higher morale, motivation, and commitment.[19]

They recast the five domains as four domains (self-awareness, self-management, social awareness, and relationship management) and the 25 competencies as 18 competencies. "These...competencies are not innate talents, but learned abilities, each of which has a unique contribution to making leaders more resonant, and therefore more effective."[20] Self-awareness and self-management are personal competencies, which "determine how we manage ourselves," whereas self-awareness and relationship management are social competencies, which "determine how we manage relationships."[21] The four domains are "closely intertwined, with a dynamic relationship among them."[22]

More recently, Goleman returned to the topic of social intelligence, of which emotional intelligence is a part, and the importance of nurturing interpersonal relationships and emotions. As he notes, we can all connect better with others by developing rapport and empathy with others, while identifying personality types that have destructive influences. Clearly, social and emotional intelligence can be learned, and parents can start the teaching process early on.[23]

RESEARCH ON EMOTIONAL INTELLIGENCE

The following discussion of the research literatures reported in dissertations and peer-reviewed journals is extensive but not comprehensive.[24] It shows the types of studies conducted and highlights the findings of works both supporting and not supporting the application of EI to management and leadership.

The body of research has examined members of different populations (e.g., teachers and school principals, business people, workers and supervisors in manufacturing organizations, military personnel such as midshipmen or individuals in an officer development system, students, and leaders in both profit and non-profit organizations). It has, however, investigated a workforce mostly made up of Caucasians; in one instance, the subjects were African Americans.[25] The studies have either looked at both men and women, or focused on one gender. EI is not an exclusionary leadership style. Some of the research has linked it to transformational leadership, which centers on change management and the development of leaders who are intuitive and flexible and who nurture an organization's capacity to adapt to an unknown future.

EI also applies to teams and the ongoing development of both leaders and followers. Finally, not all of the research supports the utility of the concept as a freestanding theory. Some investigators and theorists, for instance, question the extent to which EI is linked to effectiveness, job satisfaction, and transformational leadership, whereas others concur with Goleman, Boyatzis, and McKee that EI is a critical component of effective leadership that applies to leaders and affects members of teams. Critics charge that researchers rely too much on observable characteristics and that they do not address moral and emotional concerns[26] when they seek to identify those factors that explain the success of leaders and organizations.

Dissertations

Leadership, which is an essential element in determining organizational climate as well as productivity,[27] is a major research area of doctoral dissertations, be they for the PhD or EdD. A number of those dissertations in the United States and elsewhere (e.g., Australia, Canada, Hong Kong, Singapore, South Africa, and the United Kingdom) have examined EI and its ability to explain leadership effectiveness. For example, in a study of school principals in Montana, Charles R. Cook "supports the body of research that emotional intelligence has a positive effect on leadership performance. Effective leadership requires a wide range of skills," and with it school principals can see that the educational needs of students are effectively met.[28]

Lisa Johnson identifies EI as one factor contributing to the success of women in leadership positions,[29] and Mary K. Campbell finds a positive correlation between EI and responsible risk-taking, intuition, and innovation.[30] Judith Macrae documents an increase in the EI of middle managers in healthcare. They exhibited heightened self-awareness, experienced behavioral changes, and managed positive changes in their actual leadership.[31] Mary Frances Long Gardner argues that leaders may be unaware of the emotional intelligence they project. They need an accurate understanding of their EI and guidance in achieving it. Organizations should nurture the development of emotional intelligence in developing leaders as well as make a commitment to its development among the professional staff.[32]

Mark E. Burbach finds that "the leader's internal self-concept moderates the relationship between emotional intelligence and transformational leadership, contingent reward leadership and outcomes of leadership from rater's perceptions." He concludes that there is "guarded optimism for the predictive value of an ability model of emotional intelligence in leadership research."[33] In another important study, Gina Buontempo explores the relationship between EI and decision making. She finds "various differential relationships" between EI and particular skills (namely self-awareness, creativity, and empathy), which affect heuristic-based judgment biases (e.g., over-confidence, ease of recall, and false consensus). Without EI and the above-mentioned skills, ineffective decision making might occur.[34]

Not all of the dissertations find an association between EI and leadership effectiveness. These researchers suggest that emotional intelligence does not necessarily contribute to organizational or individual performance, transformational leadership, or the success of those executives studied.[35]

The Social Sciences

Cary Cherniss provides a good introduction to EI and relevant research, showing that "there was a long tradition of research on the role of non-cognitive factors in helping people to succeed in both life and the workplace. The current work on emotional intelligence builds on this foundation." He shows that EI "has as much to do with knowing when and how to express emotion as it does with controlling it" and that empathy, an important aspect of EI, "contributes to occupational success." Cherniss inserts an important reminder that by itself emotional intelligence probably is not a strong predictor of job performance. Rather, it provides the bedrock for competencies that are. Goleman has tried to represent this idea by making a distinction between emotional intelligence and emotional competence. Emotional competence refers to the personal and social skills that lead to superior performance in the world of work. The emotional competencies are linked to and based on emotional intelligence. A certain level of emotional intelligence is necessary to learn the emotional competencies. For instance, the ability to recognize accurately what another person is feeling enables one to develop a specific competency such as Influence. Similarly, people who are better able to regulate their emotions will find it easier to develop a competency such as Initiative or Achievement drive. Ultimately it is these social and emotional competencies that we need to identify and measure if we want to be able to predict performance.[36]

Chi-Sum Wong and Kenneth S. Law, along with Lynda L. Song, advance their own theoretical perspectives on emotional intelligence and show that the measures they consider have favorable psychometric properties. They then used those measures to predict managerial outcomes. Further, they explained unique variance, the spread of the scores around the mean, after controlling for widely accepted personality variables.[37] Steven B. Wolf, Anthony T. Pescosolido, and Vanessa U. Druskat, who used EI to explore the emergence of leadership within self-managed teams, discover that empathy is related to selection of individuals for leadership positions.[38]

James M. Kouzes and Barry Z. Posner maintain that leaders care about the feelings of others and what others think about what they say and do. They use EI to develop trust relationships by demonstrating sensitivity to the needs and interests of a leader's constituents. Further, to be credible as a leader, individuals need to "inspire a shared vision" and, among other traits, to be competent, forward thinking, and honest. Kouzes and Possner emphasize the importance of values, "the guiding principles in our lives with respect to the personal and social ends we desire." Values, they note, guide how leaders feel, what they say and think, the choices they make, and how they act.[39]

A. Langley, who underscores the importance of EI, suggests that employees mimic poor leadership traits in the same way they do a leader's positive traits. Further, if the personal and social abilities that reflect high EI can be understood and assessed, then a new perspective on management development will result and people will be able to reach their potential.[40]

In a highly cited study, Jennifer M. George maintains that emotions are critical to effective leadership. She identifies four interrelated aspects of EI that enable leaders to motivate and transform team members. First, for self-awareness, they must effectively portray personal emotion and accurately appraise the emotions of others (*the appraisal and expression of emotion*). Second, as part of the emotional regulation of team members, they must predict emotional reactions to various situations and provide positive reinforcement (*the use of emotion to enhance cognitive processes and decision making*). Third, they must also use emotions to influence the behavior and cognition of others (*knowledge about emotions*). And, finally, they must manage their own emotions and realize the impact of emotional regulation on team performance and the general interaction among the staff (*the management of emotions*).[41]

Malcolm Higgs recasts the domains advanced by Goleman into seven components:

1. self-awareness, which relates to a person's self-knowledge

2. emotional resilience, which is "the ability to perform consistently in a range of situations under pressure and to adapt one's behavior appropriately"

3. motivation, which is "the drive and energy to achieve clear results and make an impact" as well as to balance short- and long-term goals

4. interpersonal sensitivity, "which is the ability to be aware of and take account of the needs and perceptions of others when arriving at decisions and proposing solutions to problems and challenges"

5. influence, which is the ability to persuade others to change their opinions

6. intuitiveness (decisiveness), which is the ability to reach decisions based on incomplete information

7. conscientiousness, which is "the ability to display clear commitment to a course of action in the face of challenge"[42]

Subsequently, decisiveness was dropped as part of intuitiveness, and integrity was added to conscientiousness. He argues that this characterization of emotional intelligence is closely associated with advancement within an organization and that interpersonal sensitivity, influence, and self-awareness are components that can be developed.[43]

As Bernard M. Bass and Ronald E. Riggio observe, "transformational leadership is a process of evoking and managing the emotions of followers—very consistent with concepts of emotional intelligence."[44] Wendelin Kupers and Jürgen Weibler, however, view transformational leadership as a leadership style devoid of emotions, and, as a result, they see EI as adding an important dimension.[45] On the other hand, other studies show that transformational leaders possess high levels of emotional intelligence as well as heightened intuition, greater insights into complex challenges, and increased self-motivation.[46] In a study of 176 female managers in different industries in Australia, L. A. Downey, V. Papageorgiou, and C. Stough find a relationship among emotional intelligence, transformational leadership, and intuition. In particular, those participants who display more transformational leadership behaviors demonstrate higher levels of EI and intuition than those managers who show fewer of those behaviors.[47]

John J. Sosik and Lara E. Megerian discovered that EI, transformational leadership, and job performance vary as a function of a manager's self-awareness. They conclude that self-awareness might comprise the foundational competency on which other EI competencies are based.[48]

Robert S. Rubin, David C. Munz, and William H. Bommer examine how leaders' emotional recognition and personality influence their uses of transformational leadership. They find that leaders who possess high extraversional personalities and high emotion recognition also rate highly on transformational leadership.[49]

Simon Moss, Damian Ritossa, and Simon Ngu, who have also linked emotional intelligence to transformational leadership, conclude that such intelligence should enable managers "to identify employees who focus primarily on aspirations and achievements rather than duties and obligations.... [Managers] should divert their attention from the errors these employees commit and, instead, focus on recent accomplishments and future objectives." As a result, "extroverts are more sensitive to rewards, not punishments, and, thus, feel less commitment when their leaders are critical or detached."[50]

F. William Brown, Scott E. Bryant, and Michael D. Reilly examine 2,411 manufacturing workers, engineers, and professional staff. They support the importance of transformational leadership in the achievement of organizational outcomes. However, they do not find a statistically significant relationship between emotional intelligence and transformational leadership, or between emotional intelligence and organizational outcomes. They conclude that EI "may be a useful concept in understanding leadership and social influence"; however, unlike some previous studies, they offer no indication that EI "as operationalized and measured by the EQI [Bar-On Emotional Quotient Inventory] is of particular value in that exploration."[51] Instead of casting doubts about the validity of EI, they question the use of EQI as a means of data collection.

In a different study, F. William Brown and Dan Moshavi add to the literature linking EI to transformational leadership and individual and organizational outcomes. They suggest that, to some extent, non-cognitive emotional intelligence might explain interpersonal influence and leadership; however, before it can do so, significant issues of definition, psychometric independence, and measurement must be resolved.[52]

A number of researchers have shown that EI plays a key role in the work environment. Thomas Sy, Susanna Tram, and Linda A. O'Hara examine "the relationships among employees' emotional intelligence, their managers' emotional intelligence, employees' job satisfaction, and performance for 187 food service employees from nine different locations of the same restaurant franchise." Among their findings were that employers with higher EI "have job satisfaction," managers "with higher EI are more adept at using their emotions to facilitate job performance, and "employees with high EI are more adept at identifying and regulating their emotions." As they discuss,

the ability to understand their emotions could imply that employees with high EI are more aware of the factors that contribute to their experience of positive and negative emotions. Accordingly, awareness of the factors that elicit certain emotions and understanding the effects of those emotions enable employees with high EI to take the appropriate actions that influence job satisfaction.[53]

In a related study, Marie T. Dasborough finds that "leader behaviors were sources of positive or negative emotional responses in employees; employees recalled more negative incidents than positive incidents, and they recalled them more intensely and in more detail than positive incidents." She concludes that effective leaders manage their emotions and that they may need to exercise their emotional intelligence to generate emotional uplifts to overcome the hassles in the workplace that employees seem to remember so vividly.[54]

Robert Kerr, John Garvin, Norma Heaton, and Emily Boyle, who examine supervisors in a manufacturing firm, recommend the use of EI in the recruitment and selection of managers as well as in their training and development.[55] In another study, Ilan Alon and James M. Higgins point out that cross-cultural leadership and programs of leadership development in multinational firms must develop "culturally attuned and emotionally sensitive global leaders." As a result, the importance of cultural intelligence to transferring "emotional intelligence to other nations/cultures" should not be underestimated.[56]

J. Lee Whittington, Tricia M. Pitts, Woody V. Kagler, and Vicki L. Goodwin link EI to spiritual and biblically based approaches to leadership. They identify the leadership traits of the Apostle Paul and believe that those traits are useful in changing the lives of followers. By drawing some parallels between those traits and emotional intelligence, they conclude that "emotional intelligence should be considered within the context of legacy leadership."[57]

Ellen Paek, who links religiosity with EI, discovered that "religious attitudes were more strongly predictive of perceived EI than were religious behaviors." Further, emotional understanding was the most prominent component of EI among 148 church-attending adult Christians.[58]

Library and Information Science

The research on EI appearing in the literature of library and information science is limited. Peter Hernon and Nancy Rossiter refocused the body of research performed by Hernon, Ronald R. Powell, and Arthur P. Young on the attributes that academic and public library directors of the future will need to possess.[59] That recasting of attributes adheres to the five categories that Goleman first advanced. Hernon and Rossiter, who surveyed directors of libraries with membership in the Association of Research Libraries, found that the most prized attribute among all categories was "visionary—able to build a shared vision and rally others around it," followed by the "ability to function in a political environment."[60] They conclude that an emotionally intelligent leader appears to have much in common with a transformational leader.[61] Clearly, some traits are more important than others, and they encourage others to pare down the list.

Because leaders who serve as chief executives may find it difficult to sustain their effectiveness over time, given the "unprecedented challenges that can result in a vicious cycle of stress, pressure, sacrifice, and dissonance,"[62] resonant leadership is an important companion theory. Applying to those leaders who have developed their EI and who are in tune with those around them, resonant leadership addresses "renewal or developing practices—habits of mind, body, and behavior—that enable us to create and sustain resonance in the face of unending challenges, year in and year out."[63] Leaders renew or restore themselves—and others—by "cultivating skills and practices that will counter the effects of our stressful roles,"[64] and resonant leadership ensures that leaders remain focused on power and influence, without losing contact with others.

As McKee, Frances Johnston, and Richard Massimilian point out,

> When leaders face power stress over the long term and cannot find ways to manage its downside, they risk becoming trapped in the Sacrifice Syndrome, a vicious circle leading to mental and physical distress, and sometimes even executive burnout. . . . [They] may find that things begin to slip at work and/or at home: small problems may seem more than usually troublesome; relationships may become strained; self-confidence may slip and physical health may suffer as well. Some people may even begin to act out; they may make rash decisions, act impulsively or do things that seem to contradict their values.[65]

Cheryl Metoyer and Hernon examined resonant leadership among academic library directors who are African Americans, Hispanics, and Native Americans, and who are recognized leaders (see chapter 9). Those directors completed a diary, which is "a kind of self-administered questionnaire . . . [that] places a great deal of responsibility on the respondent."[66] They found that the directors set aside time every day to engage in renewal. The diary method documents their focus on mindfulness, at least that portion that centers on themselves and not how others perceive them. The method showed the importance of reflection and supportive relationships. There is a direct relationship between mindfulness and physical exercise. The exercise enables them to stay mentally and physically alert as well as to feel relaxed and re-energized. Diary entries indicate that the directors do not display some of the signs of the Sacrifice Syndrome. They do this by:

- attending functions or games for their children
- avoiding getting home later or leaving home earlier each day
- cooking
- discussing problems and issues with their partners
- engaging in prayer and meditation

- exercising on a regular basis
- falling asleep without any problems
- finding time for the things they find enjoyable
- having conversations with a friend or family member

Finally, Hernon and Rossiter edited *Making a Difference,* which examines leadership in academic libraries.[67] Emotional intelligence comprises an important part of the discussion, as does transformational leadership. Returning to the five domains that Goleman first articulated, they offer a 360-degree assessment tool applicable to managerial leaders in academic libraries (see chapter 15).

The Detractors

In response to L. Melita Prati, Ceasar Douglas, Gerald R. Ferris, Anthony P. Ammeter, and M. Ronald Buckley, who argue there is a positive relationship between EI and leadership,[68] John Antonakis of the University of Lausanne (Switzerland) summarizes the literature critical of EI as a predictor of leadership effectiveness. He charges that a number of the claims are "exaggerated" and questions whether emotional intelligence is "vital for leadership." "Indeed," he writes, "there is very little empirical evidence published in scientific journals indicating that EI is necessary for leadership effectiveness when controlling for personality variables or general intelligence, especially at top leader levels using *practicing leaders.*"[69] Furthermore "empirical evidence demonstrating that EI explains a large portion of the variance in leader emergence or effectiveness is non-existent or very weak at best and contradictory at worst."[70]

Other criticisms center on the belief that the competencies associated with the mixed model comprise a mixture of actions, skills, and traits and not a coherent, well-defined theoretical concept;[71] the analysis of EI through self-reporting instruments creates the possibility of non-sampling error;[72] and accepting an individual's self-assessment is similar to asking someone to self-identify his or her level of cognitive intelligence.[73]

Neal M. Ashkanasy and Catherine S. Daus list "the following 'safe' four-point summary of views on emotional intelligence":

1. distinct from, but positively related to, other types of intelligence
2. an individual difference with which some people are more endowed than others
3. developing over one's career and enhanced through training
4. involving a person's abilities in part to identify and perceive emotions in oneself and others, as well as to possess the skills necessary to understand and manage those emotions successfully[74]

Jeffrey M. Conte agrees but argues that there is a need for improvement in the conceptualization of EI, the methodologies used to examine it, and the assessment tools used.[75] Moshe Zeidner, Gerald Matthews, and Richard D. Roberts caution that "the ratio of hyperbole to hard evidence is high, with over-reliance in the literature on expert opinion, anecdote, case studies, and unpublished proprietary surveys."[76]

DATA COLLECTION INSTRUMENTS USED TO MEASURE EMOTIONAL INTELLIGENCE

The research has relied on assorted data collection instruments, each of which should be reviewed before use for the discussion of their validity and the model that they support. Over time, the various instruments have been modified, revised, and refined, thereby making longitudinal comparisons impossible.

Robert Kerr, John Garvin, Norma Heaton, and Emily Boyle review different instruments and relate them to abilities and mixed models of emotional intelligence.[77] For instance, the Bar-On Emotional Quotient Inventory EQ-i, which Bar-On developed, has been in use for more than a decade. Consisting of 133 items, it measures various constructs related to EI.[78] The Educational Leadership Improvement Tool, which The Wallace Foundation and the University of Oregon developed, can be used for "self-assessment, peer evaluation, or 360-degree review, as well as scoring guides for categories such as leadership attributes, data-driven improvement, organization, management, and cultural competence."[79]

The Emotional Competence Inventory (ECI), which is a 360-degree assessment tool designed to assess EI, is available from the Hay Group, a global management consulting company.[80] The Emotional Intelligence Appraisal, another 360-degree assessment tool, corresponds to Goleman's four-domain conception of EI. It "is available in both self-report, multi-rater, and team formats."[81]

The Emotional Intelligence Questionnaire: Managerial offers both self-report and 360-degree applications, "with the latter enabling an all-round assessment of an individual's performance from peers, colleagues and manager." The Emotional Intelligence Questionnaire assesses "an individual's potential based around seven scales":

1. self-awareness

2. emotional resilience

3. motivation

4. interpersonal sensitivity

5. influence

6. intuitiveness

7. conscientiousness[82]

The Mayer-Salovey-Caruso Emotional Intelligence Test (MSCEIT) is "an ability-based scale that measures how well people perform tasks and solve emotional problems."[83] "A Psychometric Evaluation of the Mayer-Salovey-Caruso Emotional Intelligence Test Version 2.0" is an excellent review of the psychometric properties of different instruments for measuring EI.[84]

CONCLUSION

Leadership, which has been studied more extensively than almost any other aspect of human behavior,[85] deals with setting and working toward the accomplishment of a shared vision, mission, and goals. It involves social interaction in which leaders influence the behavior and performance of their followers, and empower others to act on the vision and mission. Leaders also seek to understand and manage their own emotions and to improve their ability to lead and to deal with other leaders. Leadership is therefore "intrinsically an emotional process, whereby leaders recognize followers' emotional states, attempt to evoke emotions in followers, and then seek to manage followers' emotional states accordingly."[86] Central to leadership is a willingness to share what one knows or has learned with others in the organization.

Despite the inconsistent research record and the fact that the concept "remains the subject of some controversy and challenge,"[87] most of the studies have shown that EI is a component of transformational leadership. It has significant promise as a construct separate from personality traits, and it is necessary for leaders engaged in change management to possess. The authors of this book concur with Ashkanasy and Daus, who "posit that emotional intelligence research will continue to be a central plank of organizational behavior research for the foreseeable future."[88]

"The fundamental task of leaders... is to prime good feeling in those they lead."[89]

NOTES

1. Daniel Goleman, "What Makes a Leader?" *Harvard Business Review* 82, no. 1 (January 2004): 82. This article originally appeared in the *Harvard Business Review* 76, no. 6 (November/December 1998): 93–102.

2. Wikipedia, "Emotional Intelligence," http://en.wikipedia.org/wiki/Emotional_intelligence (accessed December 6, 2006).

3. Peter Salovey and John D. Mayer, "Emotional Intelligence," *Imagination, Cognition, and Personality* 9 (1990): 189.

4. John D. Mayer and Peter Salovey, "What Is Emotional Intelligence," in *Emotional Development and Emotional Intelligence: Educational Implications*, ed. Peter Salovey and David J. Sluyter (New York: Basic Books, 1997), 10.

5. Howard Gardner, *Multiple Intelligence: The Theory in Practice* (New York: Basic Books, 1993).

6. Wayne L. Payne, *A Study of Emotion: Developing Emotional Intelligence, Self-integration, Relating to Fear, Pain and Desire (Theory, Structure of Reality,*

Problem-solving, Contraction/expansion, Tuning in/comingout/letting Go) (doctoral diss., The Union for Experimenting Colleges and Universities [now The Union Institute], 1985). Available from *Dissertations & Theses: Full Text,* AAT 8605928.

7. Daniel Goleman, *Emotional Intelligence* (New York: Bantam Books, 1995). As Neal M. Ashkanasy and Catherine S. Daus point out, "*New York Times* social science journalist Daniel Goleman, who was researching for a book on 'emotional literacy' in education, came across Mayer and Salovey's work and decided to rename his book *Emotional Intelligence: Why It Can Matter More Than IQ,* which was published in 1995. It is now a matter of history that this became a bestseller, including a *Time Magazine* cover feature...and brought emotional intelligence to the forefront of public attention." Neal M. Ashkanasy and Catherine S. Daus, "Rumors of the Death of Emotional Intelligence in Organizational Behavior Are Vastly Exaggerated," *Journal of Organizational Behavior* 26 (2005): 442.

8. See John D. Mayer and Peter Salovey, "The Intelligence of Emotional Intelligence," *Intelligence* 17 (1993): 433–42; Salovey and Mayer, "Emotional Intelligence;" John D. Mayer and others, "Emotional Intelligence as a Standard Intelligence," *Emotion* 1 (2001): 232–42.

For an introduction to the work of David McClelland, see Accel-Team, "Human Relations Contributors: David McClelland," http://www.accel-team.com/human_relations/hrels_06_mcclelland.html (accessed December 30, 2006).

Perhaps the best historical and most critical perspective on emotional intelligence appears in Gerald Matthews, Moshe Zeidner, and Richard D. Roberts, *Emotional Intelligence: Science and Myth* (Cambridge, MA: The MIT Press, 2002). This source provides a bibliography of approximately 90 pages on the topic.

9. Victor Dulewicz and Malcolm Higgs, "Emotional Intelligence: A Review and Evaluation Study," *Journal of Managerial Psychology* 15, no. 4 (2000): 341–72. See also Claude Steiner, *Achieving Emotional Literacy* (New York: Avon Books, 1997); Robert K. Cooper, "Applying Emotional Intelligence in the Workplace," *Training & Development* 51, no. 12 (December 1997): 31–8; Gardner, *Multiple Intelligence;* Howard Gardner and Thomas Hatch, "Multiple Intelligences Go to School: Educational Implications of the Theory of Multiple Intelligences," *Educational Researcher* 18, no. 8 (1989): 4–9.

10. See John D. Mayer, *Emotional Intelligence Information: A Site Dedicated to Communicating Scientific Information about Emotional Intelligence, Including Relevant Aspects of Emotions, Cognition, and Personality,* http://www.unh.edu/emotional_intelligence/ (accessed December 28, 2006).

11. Salovey and Mayer, "Emotional Intelligence," 186. Mayer and Salovey, "The Intelligence of Emotional Intelligence;" Mayer and Salovey, "What Is Emotional Intelligence." See also Barbara Mandell and Shilpa Pherwani, "Relationship between Emotional Intelligence and Transformational Leadership Style: A Gender Comparison," *Journal of Business & Psychology* 17, no. 3 (2003): 389.

12. Kenneth S. Law, Chi-Sum Wong, and Lynda L. Song, "The Construct and Criterion Validity of Emotional Intelligence and Its Potential Utility for Management Studies," *Journal of Applied Psychology* 89, no. 3 (2004): 484.

13. Goleman, *Emotional Intelligence;* Daniel Goleman, *Working with Emotional Intelligence* (New York: Bantam Books, 1998); Reuven Bar-On, *Bar-On Emotional Quotient Inventory: Technical Manual* (Toronto: Multi Health Systems, 1997).

For an excellent review of both models, see Robert J. Emmerling and Daniel Goleman, "Emotional Intelligence: Issues and Common Misunderstanding" (Rutgers University, The Consortium for Research on Emotional Intelligence in Organizations, 2003), http://www.eiconsortium.org/research/EI_Issues_And_Common_Misunder standings.pdf (accessed December 30, 2006); Moshe Zeidner, Gerald Matthews, and Richard D. Roberts, "Emotional Intelligence in the Workplace: A Critical Review," Applied Psychology: An International Review 53, no. 3 (2004): 371–99; Ronald E. Riggio, Susan E. Murphy, and Francis J. Pirozzolo, Multiple Intelligences and Leadership (Mahwah, NJ: Lawrence Erlbaum Associates, 2002), 56–63.

14. Goleman, *Emotional Intelligence,* 317.

15. Ibid., 150–54.

16. Goleman, *Working with Emotional Intelligence.*

17. Goleman, "What Makes a Leader?" 82–91.

18. Ibid., 91.

19. Daniel Goleman, Richard Boyatzis, and Annie McKee, *Primal Leadership: Realizing the Power of Emotional Intelligence* (Boston, MA: Harvard Business School Press, 2002), 5.

20. Ibid., 38.

21. Ibid., 39.

22. Ibid., 30.

23. Daniel Goleman, *Social Intelligence: The New Science of Human Relationships* (New York: Bantam, 2006).

24. In an edited work, 25 contributors provide a complementary discussion of the research into emotional intelligence and identify numerous other studies. They document the progress made in defining and measuring linkages between emotional competence and work performance. A person's emotions influence how he or she perceives and interprets information and how he or she responds to others. See Vanessa Urch Druskat, Fabio Sala, and Gerald Mount, eds., *Linking Emotional Intelligence and Performance at Work: Current Research Evidence with Individuals and Groups* (Mahwah, NJ: Lawrence Erlbaum Associates, 2006).

25. See, e.g., Terry Yancey-Bragg, *Leadership Theories, Perceptions and Assessments: The Relationship of African American Women in a Fortune 500 Company* (Doctoral diss., Wilmington College, 2006). Available from *Dissertations & Theses: Full Text,* AAT 3189966.

26. See Janet B. Kellett, Ronald H. Humphrey, and Randall G. Sleeth, "Empathy and the Emergence of Task and Relations Leaders," *The Leadership Quarterly* 17 (2006): 158; F. William Brown, Scott E. Bryant, and Michael D. Reilly, "Does Emotional Intelligence—as Measured by the EQI—Influence Transformational Leadership and/or Desirable Outcomes?" *Leadership & Organization Development Journal* 27, no. 5 (2006): 330–51.

27. Sheila Rogers Gerrish, *A Study of the Relationship of Principal Emotional Intelligence Competencies to Middle School Organizational Climate and Health in the State of Washington* (Doctoral diss., Seattle Pacific University, 2005). Available from *Dissertations & Theses: Full Text,* AAT 3178673.

28. Charles R. Cook, *Effects of Emotional Intelligence on Principals' Leadership Performance* (Doctoral diss., Montana State University, Bozeman, 2006). Available from *Dissertations & Theses: Full Text,* AAT 3206272.

29. Lisa Johnson, *An Analysis of Major Facilitators to Their Success as Reported by Successful Women Administrators* (Doctoral diss., East Tennessee State University, 2005). Available from *Dissertations & Theses: Full Text*, AAT 3195376.

30. Mary K. Campbell, *Exploring the Relationship between Emotional Intelligence, Intuition, and Responsible Risk-taking in Organizations* (Doctoral diss., California School of Professional Psychology, 2000). Available from *Dissertations & Theses: Full Text*, AAT 9997529.

31. Judith Macrae, *Self-awareness: The Missing Link to Leadership?* (Doctoral diss., Royal Roads University (Canada), 2004). Available from *Dissertations & Theses: Full Text*, AAT MQ93750.

32. Mary Frances L. Gardner, *An Analysis of a Woman Administrator's Leadership Competency Behaviors* (Doctoral diss., University of Arkansas, 2004). Available from *Dissertations & Theses: Full Text*, AAT 3158061.

33. Mark E. Burbach, *Testing the Relationship between Emotional Intelligence and Full-range Leadership as Moderated by Cognitive Style and Self-concept* (Doctoral diss., University of Nebraska, Lincoln, 2004), unpaged. Available from *Dissertations & Theses: Full Text*, AAT 31269944.

34. Gina Buontempo, *Emotional Intelligence and Decision Making: The Impact of Judgment Biases* (Doctoral diss., Columbia University, 2005). Available from *Dissertations & Theses: Full Text*, AAT 3174752.

35. See, for instance, Lisa A. Weinberger, *An Examination of the Relationship between Emotional Intelligence, Leadership Style and Perceived Leadership Effectiveness* (Doctoral diss., University of Minnesota, 2003). Available from *Dissertations & Theses: Full Text*, AAT 3113218; Melanie J. Schulte, *Emotional Intelligence: A Predictive or Descriptive Construct in Ascertaining Leadership Style or a New Name for Old Knowledge?* (Doctoral diss., Our Lady of the Lake University, 2003). Available from *Dissertations & Theses: Full Text*, AAT 33068435; Virginia L. Collins, *Emotional Intelligence and Leadership Success* (Doctoral diss., University of Nebraska, Lincoln, 2001). Available from *Dissertations & Theses: Full Text*, AAT 3034371; Renée M. Smith, *An Examination of the Relationship between Emotional Intelligence and Leader Effectiveness* (Doctoral diss., Nova Southeastern University, 2006). Available from *Dissertations & Theses: Full Text*, AAT 3205547.

36. Cary Cherniss, "Emotional Intelligence: What It Is and Why It Matters" (paper presented at the Annual Meeting of the Society for Industrial and Organizational Psychology, New Orleans, LA, April 15, 2000), http://www.eiconsortium. org/research/what_is_emotional_intelligence.htm (accessed December 30, 2006).

37. Chi-Sum Wong and Kenneth S. Law, "The Effect of Leader and Follower Emotional Intelligence on Performance and Attitude: An Exploratory Study," *The Leadership Quarterly* 13, no. 3 (June 2002): 243–74; Law, Wong, and Song, "Construct and Criterion Validity of Emotional Intelligence."

38. Steven B. Wolf, Anthony T. Pescosolido, and Vanessa U. Druskat, "Emotional Intelligence as the Basis of Leadership Emergence in Self-managing Teams," *Leadership Quarterly* 13, no. 5 (2002): 505–22.

39. See James M. Kouzes and Barry Z. Posner, *Encouraging the Heart: A Leader's Guide to Rewarding and Recognizing Others* (San Francisco: Jossey-Bass, 1999), xiii, 10; James M. Kouzes and Barry Z. Posner, *Credibility: How Leaders Gain and Lose It, and Why People Demand It* (San Francisco: Jossey-Bass, 1993), 60.

40. Andrew Langley, "Emotional Intelligence—A New Evaluation for Management Development," *Career Development International* 5, no. 3 (2000): 177–83.

41. Jennifer M. George, "Emotions and Leadership: The Role of Emotional Intelligence," *Human Relations* 53, no. 8 (2000): 1027–44.

42. Malcolm Higgs, "Is There a Relationship between the Myers-Briggs Type Indicator and Emotional Intelligence?" *Journal of Managerial Psychology* 16, no. 7 (2001): 518–19.

43. Ibid., 519. See also Malcolm Higgs, "Do Leaders Need Emotional Intelligence? A Study of the Relationship between Emotional Intelligence and Leadership of Change," *International Journal of Organisational Behaviour* 5, no. 6 (2002): 201.

44. Bernard M. Bass and Ronald E. Riggio, *Transformational Leadership*, 2nd ed. (Mahwah, NJ: Lawrence Erlbaum Associates, 2006).

45. Wendelin Kupers and Jürgen Weibler, "How Emotional Is Transformational Leadership Really?" *Leadership & Organization Development Journal* 27, no. 5 (2006): 368–83.

46. See L. A. Downey, V. Papageorgiou, and C. Stough, "Examining the Relationship between Leadership, Emotional Intelligence, and Intuition in Senior Female Managers," *Leadership & Organization Development Journal* 27, no. 4 (2006): 250–64.

47. Ibid., 250.

48. John J. Sosik and Lara E. Megerian, "Understanding Leader Emotional Intelligence and Performance: The Role of Self-other Agreement on Transformational Leadership Perceptions," *Group & Organization Management* 24, no. 3 (September 1999): 367–90.

49. Robert S. Rubin, David C. Munz, and William H. Bommer, "Leading from Within: The Effects of Emotion Recognition and Personality on Transformational Leadership Behavior," *Academy of Management Journal* 48, no. 5 (2005): 845–58.

50. Simon Moss, Damian Ritossa, and Simon Ngu, "The Effect of Follower Regulatory Focus and Extroversion of Leadership Behavior: The Role of Emotional Intelligence," *Journal of Individual Differences* 27, no. 2 (June 2006): 104–05.

51. Brown, Bryant, and Reilly, "Does Emotional Intelligence Influence Leadership," 330.

52. F. William Brown and Dan Moshavi, "Transformational Leadership and Emotional Intelligence: A Potential Pathway for an Increased Understanding of Interpersonal Influence," *Journal of Organizational Behavior* 26, no. 7 (November 2005): 867–71.

53. See Thomas Sy, Susanna Tram, and Linda A. O'Hara, "Relation of Employee and Managerial Emotional Intelligence to Job Satisfaction and Performance," *Journal of Vocational Behavior* 68 (2006): 461, 470.

54. Marie T. Dasborough, "Cognitive Asymmetry in Employee Emotional Reactions to Leadership Behaviors," *The Leadership Quarterly* 17 (2006): 163.

55. Robert Kerr and others, "Emotional Intelligence and Leadership Effectiveness," *Leadership & Organization Development Journal* 27, no. 4 (April 2006): 265–79.

56. Ilan Alon and James M. Higgins, "Global Leadership Success through Emotional and Cultural Intelligences," *Business Horizons* 48 (2005): 501, 505.

57. J. Lee Whittington and others, "Legacy Leadership: The Leadership Wisdom of the Apostle Paul," *The Leadership Quarterly* 16 (2005): 766.

58. Ellen Paek, "Religiosity and Perceived Emotional Intelligence among Christians," *Personality and Individual Differences* 41 (2006): 488.

59. Peter Hernon and Nancy Rossiter, "Emotional Intelligence: Which Traits Are Most Prized?" *College & Research Libraries* 67, no. 3 (May 2006): 260–75; Peter Hernon, Ronald R. Powell, and Arthur P. Young, *The Next Library Leadership: Attributes of Academic and Public Library Directors* (Westport, CT: Libraries Unlimited, 2003).

60. Hernon and Rossiter, "Emotional Intelligence," 271–72.

61. Ibid., 272.

62. Richard Boyatzis and Annie McKee, *Resonant Leadership: Renewing Yourself and Connecting with Others through Mindfulness, Hope, and Compassion* (Boston: Harvard Business School Press, 2005), 9.

63. Ibid., 5.

64. Ibid.

65. Annie McKee, Frances Johnston, and Richard Massimilian, "Mindfulness, Hope, and Compassion: A Leader's Road Map to Renewal," *Ivey Business Journal* 70, no. 5 (May/June 2006): 1. Available from General BusinessFile ASAP.

66. Colin Robson, *Real World Research: A Resource for Social Scientists and Practitioner-Researchers* (Oxford, UK: Blackwell, 1993), 254. For more about the use of a diary as a means of data collection, see Peter Hernon, Ronald R. Powell, and Arthur P. Young, "Academic Library Directors: What Do They Do?" *College & Research Libraries* 65, no. 6 (Nov. 2004): 539–40.

67. Peter Hernon and Nancy Rossiter, eds., *Making a Difference: Leadership and Academic Libraries* (Westport, CT: Libraries Unlimited, 2007).

68. L. Melita Prati and others, "Emotional Intelligence Leadership Effectiveness, and Team Outcomes," *The International Journal of Organizational Analysis* 11, no. 1 (2003): 21–40.

69. John Antonakis, "Why 'Emotional Intelligence' Does not Predict Leadership Effectiveness: A Comment on Prati, Douglas, Ferris, Ammeter, and Buckley (2003)," *The International Journal of Organizational Analysis* 11, no. 4 (2003): 353, 357.

70. Ibid., 359. See also Wikipedia, "Emotional Intelligence," 3–4.

71. For a summary of the research on, and historical emergence of, EI, see Ashkanasy and Daus, "Rumors of the Death of Emotional Intelligence." They refer to a number of the detractors but conclude "that emotional intelligence research is grounded in recent scientific advances in the study of emotion, specifically regarding the role emotion plays in organizational behavior" (p. 441). They support the continuation of research on EI because it is important to study the way that members of organizations "perceive, understand, and mange their emotions" (p. 441).

72. K. V. Petrides and Adrian Furham, "On the Dimensional Structure of Emotional Intelligence," *Personality and Individual Differences* 29, no. 2 (August 2000): 313–20; Zeidner, Matthews, and Roberts, "Emotional Intelligence in the Workplace."

73. Zeidner, Matthews, and Roberts, "Emotional Intelligence in the Workplace."

74. Neal M. Ashkanasy and Catherine S. Daus, "Emotion in the Workplace: The New Challenge for Managers," *Academy of Management Executive* 16 (2002): 81.

75. Jeffrey M. Conte, "A Review and Critique of Emotional Intelligence Measures," *Journal of Organizational Behavior* 26, no.4 (2005): 433–40.

76. Zeidner, Matthews, and Roberts, "Emotional Intelligence in the Workplace," 371.

77. Kerr and others, "Emotional Intelligence and Leadership Effectiveness." See also Zeidner, Matthews, and Roberts, "Emotional Intelligence in the Workplace."

78. The Consortium for Research on Emotional Intelligence in Organizations, *Bar-On Emotional Quotient Inventory EQ-i,* http://www.eiconsortium.org/measures/eqi.htm (accessed December 8, 2006).

79. The Wallace Foundation Education Leadership Action Network, *Educational Leadership Improvement Tool,* http://www.wallacefoundation.org/ELAN/TR/KnowledgeCategories/DevelopingLeaders/PerfMeasurement/ed_ldr_improvement_tool.htm (accessed December 8, 2006). The Swinburne University Emotional Intelligence Test is derived from the Bar-On Emotional Quotient Inventory. See "Emotional Intelligence and Adolescent Classroom Behaviour," http://www.swinburne.edu.au/lss/bsi/eiu/currentei.htm (accessed December 20, 2006).

80. Hay Group®, *Emotional Competency Inventory (ECI),* http://www.hayresourcesdirect.haygroup.com/Competency/Assessments_Surveys/Emotional_Competency_Inventory/Overview.asp (accessed December 17, 2006).

81. Consortium for Research on Emotional Intelligence in Organizations. *Emotional Intelligence Appraisal,* http://www.eiconsortium.org/measures/emotional_intelligence_appraisal.htm (accessed December 28, 2006).

82. ASE, *The Emotional Intelligence Questionnaire: Managerial & Managerial 360,* http://www.ase-solutions.co.uk/product.asp?id = 22 (accessed December 30, 2006).

83. The Consortium for Research on Emotional Intelligence in Organizations, *The Mayer-Salovey-Caruso Emotional Intelligence Test (MSCEIT),* http://www.eiconsortium.org/measures/msceit.htm (accessed December 20, 2006).

84. See Benjamin R. Palmer and others, "A Psychometric Evaluation of the Mayer-Salovey-Caruso Emotional Intelligence Test Version 2.0," *Intelligence* 33 (2005): 285–305. See also Kerr and others, "Emotional Intelligence and Leadership Effectiveness"; Richard D. Roberts and others, "Exploring the Validity of the Mayer-Salovey-Caruso Emotional Intelligence Test (MSCEIT) with Established Emotions Measures," *Emotion* 6, no. 4 (November 2006): 663–69; Palmer and others, "A Psychometric Evaluation of the Mayer-Salovey-Caruso Emotional Intelligence Test Version 2.0," ERIC EJ698156. Availability information can be found at http://eric.ed.gov/ERICWebPortal/Home.portal?_nfpb=true&_pageLabel=RecordDetails&ERICExtSearch_SearchValue_0=EJ698156&ERICExtSearch_SearchType_0=eric_accno&objectId=0900000b8034c781 (accessed December 8, 2006). For additional information about relevant instruments, see Answers.com, "Emotional Intelligence Tests." Available at http://www.answers.com/topic/emotional-intelligence-tests (accessed December 8, 2006). Karen D. Lokelani Bryson, *Managerial Success and Derailment: The Relationship between Emotional Intelligence and Leadership* (Doctoral diss., East Tennessee State University, 2005). Available from *Dissertations & Theses: Full Text,* AAT 315997.

85. Malcolm Higgs, "How Can We Make Sense of Leadership in the 21st Century?" *Leadership & Organization Development Journal* 24, no. 5 (2002): 273.

86. Kerr and others, "Emotional Intelligence and Leadership Effectiveness," 268.

87. Higgs, "Leadership in the 21st Century" 278.

88. Ashkanasy and Daus, "Rumors of the Death of Emotional Intelligence," 449.

89. Goleman, Boyatzis, and McKee, *Primal Leadership,* ix.

3

SOME VIEWS OF LIBRARY LEADERS

Joan Giesecke and Camila A. Alire

"Research shows that emotions, properly managed, can drive trust, loyalty and commitment—and many of the greatest productivity gains, innovations, and accomplishments of individuals, teams, and organizations."[1]

One of the interesting challenges in studying emotional intelligence is to determine if leaders believe the concept is important and worthy of their time and effort. Do they, even those who may demonstrate a high level of emotional intelligence, see emotional intelligence as more than the traditional people skills discussed in the management literature? Further, if leaders are task oriented, do they see value in understanding people's emotions and feelings and the impact feelings have on the organizational environment? To obtain insights complementary to the rest of this book, the authors conducted a small-scale survey.

A BRIEF SURVEY

At a 2007 national library conference, the authors asked 12 library directors whom they know and who interact effectively with others while managing their own emotional intelligence to meet with them and complete the survey (see chapter appendix). The purpose of the survey was to discover more about how library directors perceive emotional intelligence as an important leadership theory and set of traits. Do they monitor emotional responses from others in meetings, and do they think that initiative, collaboration, teamwork, commitment, self-confidence, innovation, quality, and customer service by leaders produce a positive organization? They were also asked if it is important for leaders to receive feedback from a support system of mentors and peers. Should leaders resonate energy, demonstrate mindfulness, hope, and compassion, and have ways to combat stress and burnout? This question addresses a companion leadership theory, known as resonant leadership.

Applying to those leaders who have developed their emotional intelligence and who are in tune with those around them, resonant leadership addresses "renewal or developing practices—habits of mind, body, and behavior—that enable us to create and sustain resonance in the face of unending challenges, year in and year out."[2] Leaders renew or restore themselves and others by "cultivating skills and practices that will counter the effects of...[their] stressful roles,"[3] and resonant leadership ensures that leaders remain focused on power and influence, without losing contact with others.

In the survey, the questions in the first part were measured on a five-point Likert scale ranging from *strongly agree* to *strongly disagree*. In the second part, the leaders were asked if it was important to control one's emotions, to understand emotions of staff, to watch for emotional responses in meetings, and to influence the emotions of others. The directors were also asked if they felt they could drive emotions in the right direction to have a positive impact on the organization. For these questions, an answer of true or false was sufficient. The third part contained three open-ended questions that asked what upcoming leaders need to know about managing the human side of the organization, what the leaders do when they do not feel effective, and how they handle frustration and stress. The final part of the survey elicited descriptive information about the respondents.

The Respondents

The group included three male and nine female directors. They were all in their forties or fifties. Regarding years of experience as a library director, four directors (33%) have 1 to 5 years, three (25%) have 6 to 10 years, four (33%) have 11 to 20 years, and one (8%) has more than 21 years of experience. Viewed from another perspective, eight directors (67%) have more than five years of experience as a library director.

Three directors (25%) are African American, while the rest are Caucasian. The group mostly represented larger libraries with only two directors (17%) working at institutions with fewer than 3,000 students (FTE or full-time equivalents); the other directors are evenly divided between colleges of 10,000 to 20,000 student FTE, and those from schools with more than 20,000 student FTE.

STUDY FINDINGS

Most of the answers to the survey were consistent among the group. In seven of the questions, all respondents indicated they *agreed* or *strongly agreed* with the statement. When asked to identify which characteristics set a positive tone in the library, all of them listed:

- Initiative
- Collaboration
- Commitment
- Innovation
- Quality service

There was the most disagreement that customer loyalty sets a positive tone, and respondents were split about teamwork and self-confidence.

Further, all respondents believe that effective leaders watch for emotional responses in meetings and find ways to combat stress, avoid burnout, and renew themselves physically, mentally, and emotionally. Only one respondent (8%) does not believe "it is critical that academic library deans/directors not only demonstrate emotional maturity but also understand the emotions of their staff." Likewise, one respondent does not think "academic library deans/directors can drive emotions in the right direction that can have a positive impact on their libraries."

For the following two statements, one respondent marked a neutral response whereas the others either agreed or did so strongly:

1. Emotionally intelligent academic library leaders' feedback comes from a support system that includes honest feedback from mentors, coaches, and/or peer groups
2. Leaders who resonate energy and enthusiasm have library organizations that thrive.

In one instance, one respondent marked a neutral response and another strongly disagreed:

- The following characteristics—*mindfulness, hope, and compassion*—are qualities that can create effective leadership.

There was the least agreement among the respondents regarding "if you understand the emotions of a staff member, you can effectively influence that person." Here nine respondents (75%) considered this statement to be false. Interestingly, all three of the African American respondents were among that group. There was one other statement that some respondents noted as false. Four directors (33%) do not believe that controlling one's emotions is very important for our libraries.

DISCUSSION OF SURVEY FINDINGS

The small sample of library directors yields some interesting results. Only one library director thinks emotions are not the concern of leaders.

This respondent states that organizational leaders should not be involved in emotions. Leaders should be concerned with behaviors and motivation, the person notes. The other interesting result was the response to the statement about the ability of leaders to influence the emotions of others. As previously mentioned, this is the only statement where all three African Americans disagreed. This result makes one wonder why this response occurred. With such a small sample it is impossible to generalize from the data. Still, the response from these three participants fits with the work that has been done on leadership, authenticity, and minority business leaders. In an article appearing in the *Harvard Business Review,* Sylvia Ann Hewlett, Carolyn Buck Luce, and Cornel West note that minority leaders are less likely to reveal information about themselves and their activities outside of work even though these activities build leadership skills.[4] Involvement in community groups, volunteer boards, and church activities is not likely to be discussed in the workplace when these activities are not valued by the organization. Could one hypothesize then that minority leaders are less likely to feel they can or should influence the emotions of others when they may be masking their own emotions and lives to fit into the majority culture? While this study cannot begin to answer such a question, it does raise an interesting set of issues for further study.

INDIVIDUAL INTERVIEWS

The brief survey was followed with more in-depth interviews of selected library directors. The interviews provided insights into how directors practice emotional intelligence. Three library leaders—a university librarian, a college librarian, and an academic law librarian—participated in these interviews. The group included two women and one man. All three have at least 15 years of experience as library directors. The results of these interviews were consistent. Their stories are presented as a composite interview to help disguise personal information that came out in the interview.

While the directors work in different environments, all three have to balance the culture of their own libraries with that of the larger institution or school. They work with faculty, staff, librarians, and administrators. Each group presents its own challenges and needs a different approach.

For staff, the librarian needs to understand the needs of and approaches taken by a group with the least status on campus. Wages and benefits generally do not match those of faculty. Staff are crucial for keeping the libraries open and performing many of the technical service tasks that make the collection available for use. They may relate more to the university as a whole rather than the individual libraries and may be involved in university-wide activities. For example, staff may join overall university staff as part of a group seeking increased compensation from the institution and may have written letters to the university administration. Some leaders may see such actions as disloyal and as an attempt to harm the reputation of the library director. Directors could react very harshly when staff tell them they were writing letters and are concerned about being fired. Instead, positive leaders had the ability to recognize that staff were taking appropriate actions within the university to raise their concern about their status in the institution. Positive leaders who understand emotional intelligence will be reassuring and supportive to staff. With some staff, a director might be able to joke with them about the actions taken. With others, a director needs to be calm and supportive as some staff are truly concerned and anxious about the response to their actions. Understanding which staff could joke about the situation and which ones do not joke around is an important skill for the director. All three directors note that it is important to be aware of how individuals react to possible stressful situations and to respond in ways that maintain a calm approach. They mention that leaders who do not control their own emotions in situations that may appear to be challenging the authority of the leader will not be as successful as those who control their own emotions and approach the situation from a reasoned viewpoint.

In working with librarians, directors noted the need for different approaches. They distinguished between the librarians who view their job as a nine-to-five position and those who have more of a teaching faculty and work more than 40 hours per week. For the first group, directors need to know who to push to achieve good performance and when to apply pressure. For the second group, directors discussed how their loyalty may be to the profession instead of the library. For this group directors need to find ways to keep them challenged and still focused on the work at hand. Different emotional and social skills may be employed to encourage the librarians to work together even though they have different values and approaches to the work.

Perhaps the most challenging situation in the workplace is dealing with long-term staff who have a negative view of the operation. These toxic employees make others in their unit unhappy and can create a dysfunctional unit. The process of working through negative attitudes becomes more complicated when the toxic, long-term employees also have health issues. Now the unit members are torn between not wanting the person in the unit and wanting to be supportive of an employee suffering from health problems. For the director, the problem is to balance the needs of the unit with the needs of the employee in a murky legal area. Addressing the situation as a straight performance and productivity issue may result in the person being dismissed eventually, but it will cause morale problems in the unit. Addressing the issue only in terms of the personal and personnel interactions may help the employee but can cause productivity issues and resentment by other staff who must pick up the person's work. Of course, complicating the situation is the need to protect the privacy of the employee. The directors noted that emotional intelligence skills can help one sort through these touchy situations. Being aware of one's own reactions and emotions about health issues, as well as of one's values, can help define the options available. Being authentic and establishing a positive working relationship with the other members of the unit can help staff understand that the leaders' intentions are good even when it is hard to tell if problems are being addressed. Still, these skills will not make the situation easy to resolve. It takes energy and persistence to work through complex personnel issues. Balancing one's emotional response with strategic options can help a leader survive the processes. Success comes with focusing on library programs and strategic objectives. Approaching personnel issues from the viewpoint of the impact of the situation on library services can help leaders stay focused on the larger picture while addressing the emotional issues present in a difficult personnel situation.

The directors also noted that it is important to be aware of individuals' mental and physical health to help individuals avoid burnout. An employee who becomes more emotional than expected may be having personal problems that are impacting the work place. Directors advised one-on-one conversations to determine why an employee may be reacting differently in the workplace. On the other hand, the directors noted that they stay above the petty, small personality conflicts that may arise. They remind staff that each person is different and brings different talents to the work place. When issues develop beyond minor conflicts, directors may get involved to help bring a focus to the situation and restore a good working environment.

All three directors noted that leaders who are unable to handle emotional issues or are unable to handle their own emotions will have problems in the workplace. While two of the directors noted they do not talk about emotional intelligence skills when mentoring up and coming library leaders, one director addressed the issue. The director noted that up-and-coming leaders need to be aware of emotional reactions to problems, and be very careful in how they, as leaders, are perceived. For example, getting so frustrated at a meeting that a person cries is not a good approach for a leader. No matter how frustrated one becomes, it is important to remain in control in the public setting. After a tough interaction, a leader may escape to his or her private office and vent or cry to release his or her own emotions. By handling negative emotions in private, the leader can retain the respect of his or her staff and be a positive influence in the organization. This does not mean that leaders do not show emotion. Rather it means that leaders with good emotional intelligence skills know when and how to express emotions to maintain a positive working environment.

In summary, the advice to new leaders from these directors on how to practice emotional intelligence included the following: carefully observe the environment, learn how librarians, faculty, and staff react to different situations, know your own strengths and weaknesses, and learn from others. Consulting other units on campus as appropriate and talking through issues with trusted colleagues are two ways to get input and ideas on how to create a successful operation in the midst of many institutional cultures and emotional environments.

A DINNER CONVERSATION AMONG LIBRARY LEADERS

Bringing six academic library leaders and two leaders in private industry together for dinner at a conference provided an unusual opportunity to explore and discuss the concepts of emotional intelligence. The group included two males and six females, all of whom held leadership positions in their organizations. The conversation took place between the appetizers and the main meal, while colleagues were relaxed and had time to chat before the main courses arrived. The conversation started with a discussion of meeting management and how often leaders think about the emotional atmosphere in a meeting setting. Interestingly, half the group felt that they often do not pay attention to the emotional atmosphere in a meeting. They are concentrating on the agenda items and getting the work done rather than being attuned to the atmosphere in the room. Further, half the group felt that they were not overly aware of their own emotional reactions, with the male colleagues feeling they were less aware of their own emotions than their female colleagues. In analyzing recent meetings, one colleague noted that a meeting with peers to accomplish a task had a different dynamic to it than a meeting of a manager and staff. In a meeting with peers, the group focused on the task at hand. When the group members were well acquainted, more humor and joking occurred during the meeting and the atmosphere was more collegial. When the group included different levels in the organization, the atmosphere was more formal and less humor was used in the meeting. It seemed that a group of peers were more attuned to each other's emotions as well as styles than was evident in a group of managers and staff.

One colleague reported that in meetings where conflicting views were expressed, and compromise did not seem to be an option, emotions were more evident. In such cases, the chair of the meeting would adjourn the meeting and ask two or three members of the group to prepare a summary of the major points of the discussion. The group would later reconvene with report in hand. Often this technique resulted in discussions that centered on the issues rather than on emotions and personalities. Progress could be made as the emotional intensity of the group was lowered. The chair of the group practiced good emotional intelligence skills without putting this label on the strategy. Instinctively the person knew how to recognize and impact the emotions of others while working to meet a group objective.

From a discussion of meetings, the group moved on to a discussion of interactions in the organizations that involved negative or toxic employees. While the dinner group members were all aware of the importance of addressing toxic behavior, they expressed the frustrations they felt when organizational processes made addressing such issues difficult. One of the greatest barriers expressed by the dinner group was that of the overall organization's human resources (HR) department. Too often they felt the human resources professional concentrated solely on job tasks in reviewing issues of poor employee performance. The HR experts were not helpful in providing guidance in how to successfully change or eliminate an employee with a poor attitude. The HR department would ask for documentation that centered on quantity and quality of work performed rather than on the impact of a negative attitude. For the dinner group, who recognized the problems created by negative employees, lack of support from the larger organization made it more difficult to employ emotional intelligence skills to resolve the problem. Their conversation on this aspect of organizational dynamics points out one of the barriers leaders face. Sometimes even the best skills cannot rectify every problem that is encountered in a complex organization. Sadly the best response to an employee problem may be to marginalize a staff member with a poor attitude and decrease the influence and impact the person has on the organization. On the other hand, colleagues in private industry reminded the group that they sometimes had more flexibility in hiring and firing and that they could more directly confront a person with a poor attitude. They cautioned however that not all organizations are attuned to the damage a toxic employee can do, and in organizations that were not cognizant of the emotional or interpersonal atmosphere, toxic employees were not in danger of losing their job.

As the conversation continued, an interesting phenomenon occurred. The individuals at the table began to analyze their own reactions. Some identified times they could be more effective if they paid attention to the impact they were having on a group. Others suggested ways they could change how they approached situations involving group interactions. They shared ideas with each other of possible strategies to use to increase the chances of success in working with others. By the time the main courses arrived, the group had moved from objectively looking at the ideas of emotional intelligence to exploring how they could be more effective as leaders by thinking about the emotional dimensions of their organizational environment.

CONCLUSION

This group of academic library directors can be categorized as possible emotionally intelligent leaders. For the most part, they view themselves as believing in the concepts and characteristics of emotional intelligence. The authors of this chapter, however, do beg the question mentioned earlier in this chapter: "Do leaders, even those who may demonstrate a high level of emotional intelligence, see emotional intelligence as more than the traditional people skills of management literature?" Maybe a more direct question might have been, "Do they consider themselves emotionally intelligent leaders?" We refrained from directly asking that question on the survey because some respondents might not have an adequate background on what emotional intelligence really is. Nor was that the purpose of the survey.

One can surmise from the results of the survey that the academic library directors' responses might have been based on their best leadership practices and common sense. Nonetheless, all but one respondent saw the value in understanding people's emotions and feelings and the impact those feelings have on the organizational environment.

Another observation is that a complementary means of data collection would be to turn some of the findings presented in this chapter into case studies and scenario plans,[5] which are stories that lay out possible futures that are not mutually exclusive and exhaustive and that help move the organization forward. Once these have been written and pre-tested, library leaders could be selected using a nonprobability sample and invited to comment. Their responses could be analyzed and presented through content analysis and concept mapping. It would seem that the methodological tool chest relevant to the study of library leadership and leadership in non-profit organizations is varied and goes beyond the reporting of survey results.

"Resonant leadership is a part of life and work. Keep personal and personnel problems in perspective. Respect others and yourself."[6]

NOTES

1. Robert K. Cooper, "Applying Emotional Intelligence in the Workplace," *Training & Development* 51, no. 12 (1997): 31.

2. Richard Boyatzis and Annie McKee, *Resonant Leadership: Renewing Yourself and Connecting with Others through Mindfulness, Hope, and Compassion* (Boston: Harvard Business School Press, 2005), 5.

3. Ibid.

4. Sylvia Ann Hewlett, Carolyn Buck Luce, and Cornel West, "Leadership in Your Midst: Tapping the Hidden Strengths of Minority Executives," *Harvard Business Review* 83, no. 11 (November, 2005): 74–82.

5. Joan Giesecke, ed., *Scenario Planning for Libraries* (Chicago: American Library Association, 1998).

6. Respondent to the survey reported in this chapter.

APPENDIX: SURVEY OF ACADEMIC LIBRARY DEANS/DIRECTORS

This survey is examining emotional intelligence or ability to interact effectively with others while managing their own emotional responses.

PART I

Please respond to the following questions/comments using the scale below:

SA	–	Strongly Agree
A	–	Agree
D	–	Disagree
SD	–	Strongly Disagree
N	–	Neutral

1. Would the following characteristics of leaders set a positive tone in your library organization?

	SA	A	D	SD	N
a. Initiative	___	___	___	___	___
b. Collaboration	___	___	___	___	___
c. Teamwork	___	___	___	___	___
d. Commitment	___	___	___	___	___
e. Self-confidence	___	___	___	___	___
f. Innovation	___	___	___	___	___
g. Quality service	___	___	___	___	___
h. Customer loyalty	___	___	___	___	___

2. Emotionally Intelligent academic library leaders' feedback comes from a support system that includes honest feedback from mentors, coaches, and/or peer groups.   ___ ___ ___ ___ ___

2. Leaders who resonate energy and enthusiasm have library organizations that thrive.   ___ ___ ___ ___ ___

3. The following characteristics—mindfulness, hope, and compassion—are qualities that can create effective leadership.   ___ ___ ___ ___ ___

4. To be effective, academic library deans/directors need to figure out ways to combat stress, avoid burnout, and renew themselves physically, mentally, and emotionally.   ___ ___ ___ ___ ___

PART II

	TRUE	FALSE
5. Given that academic libraries are service organizations, the need for controlling one's emotions is very important for our libraries.	___	___
6. It is critical that academic library deans/directors not only demonstrate emotional maturity but also understand the emotions of their staff.	___	___
7. An effective leader watches for emotional responses in meetings.	___	___

8. If you understand the emotions of a staff
member, you can effectively influence that
person.   _____   _____

9. Academic library deans/directors can drive
emotions in the right direction that can
have a positive impact on their libraries.   _____   _____

PART III. Open-ended Questions

1. What do upcoming leaders in your libraries need to know about managing the human side of the operations (i.e., the messy interactions among employees and among leaders, the emotional messes that are part of the organization)?

2. How do you cope on days when you do not feel effective?

3. How do you offset or handle frustration and stress?

PART IV. Demographics

Gender	_____Female _____Male
Age group	_____40–50 _____51–60 _____61 and over
Tenure as dean/director:	_____1–5 years _____6–10 _____11–20 _____21 and over
Race/Ethnicity	_____White _____Hispanic _____African American _____Native American _____Asian/Pacific Islander
Library Size (Student FTE)	_____3,000 or less _____3,000–10,000 _____10,000–20,000 _____Over 20,000

4

GENERAL LEADERSHIP TRAITS

Peter Hernon

"We've come to expect a lot of our leaders."[1]

Emotional intelligence is a term that has been used in various disciplines in the behavioral, medical, and social sciences, but its use is not limited to discussions of management or leadership. Emotional intelligence represents a popularized image of both management and leadership, and it informs a theory and a systematic program of research that are not fixated on intelligence as defined in terms of an intelligence quotient.

As chapter 2 indicates, the research on emotional intelligence tends to focus on one of two models: abilities or mixed models. Assorted data collection instruments address a particular model. Adhering to the writings of Daniel Goleman, the research in library and information science (LIS) is limited, but it follows the mixed model and his depiction of either five or four domains. The abilities model relies on well-defined and widely used instruments such as the Mayer-Salovey-Caruso Emotional Intelligence Test. Given the extent and variety of the research related to that model, this chapter focuses on the mixed model, which is still under refinement, especially in LIS. The chapter also examines a new framework, which addresses the distributed model of leadership; this model is not related to emotional intelligence. The purpose of this chapter therefore is to gain additional insights into assessment instruments directly related to leadership theories and styles, and whether library leaders perceive one instrument as more relevant to LIS than the other.

MAYER-SALOVEY-CARUSO EMOTIONAL INTELLIGENCE TEST

This test measures the following related abilities:

- perceiving emotions, which is the ability to identify accurately how people feel
- using emotions to facilitate thought, which is the ability to create emotions and to integrate feelings into the way people think
- understanding emotions, which refers to the ability to understand the causes of emotions
- managing emotions, which encompasses the ability to develop effective strategies for using one's emotions to achieve a goal. The purpose is to prevent someone from being influenced by his or her emotions in unpredictable ways.

David R. Caruso expands on these abilities and explains how the MSCEIT measures emotional intelligence, defined as "the ability to perceive emotions, to access and generate emotions to assist thought, to understand emotions and emotional knowledge, and to reflectively regulate emotions to promote emotional and intellectual growth."[2] Simply put, those filling out the questionnaire complete tasks such as interpreting "how much feeling is in a picture"[3] and answer questions such as "Are you always aware of your emotions?" and "Do you pay attention to others' moods?"[4] They receive a score on each of the EI abilities showing their level of competency.

According to John D. Mayer, the advantages of this questionnaire and the abilities model are that the "definition [of EI] does not include such valuable personality characteristics as achievement orientation or initiative found in the mixed model, for the simple reason that those attributes are conceptually distinct and are not directly related either to emotion or intelligence."[5]

Because instruments such as MSCEIT are well developed and amply tested, librarians might use them to view EI from the perspective of the abilities model and the body of research generated by Mayer, Peter Salovey, and others. Still, librarians may appreciate the individual characteristics included in the mixed model.

EMOTIONAL INTELLIGENCE: THE HERNON AND ROSSITER INSTRUMENT

Using the five domain characterization of emotional intelligence first developed by Goleman, Hernon and Rossiter asked academic library directors whose institutions have membership in the Association of Research Libraries to review 96 traits.[6] Respondents identified some additional traits, but they overwhelmingly selected "visionary—able to build a shared vision and rally others around it" as by far the most important. "Stable temperament and ability to maintain an emotional balance under constant tensions" was second, followed by "cognitive ability to deal with complex scenarios/situations."[7]

In the spring semester 2006, Joan Giesecke taught a course on women in leadership for the school of agriculture at the University of Nebraska–Lincoln. The students reviewed the 96 traits and considered one trait, "nurture staff" (associated with the domain of motivation), as not being gender neutral. Because they viewed nurturing usually as a female characteristic, they recommended replacement of the word "nurture" with "develop." The class also discussed how motivation in EI might be viewed as motivating either oneself or others.

Patricia Kreitz, a doctoral student in the Simmons College program in managerial leadership in the information professions, reconfigured the Hernon and Rossiter instrument into the four domains that Goleman later used.[8] With only slight modification, her instrument, which was extensively pre-tested, served as a means of collecting data for the small-scale study reported here.

The sentiment behind this chapter is that "no leader is perfect." Anyone can improve his or her skills, abilities, and knowledge, and organizations have more than one leader. Organizations are most effective when various leaders complement one another's strengths and offset one another's weaknesses.[9]

THE INVESTIGATION OF EI

This small-scale study applied a purposive sample. A purposive sampling method is one in which the researcher subjectively selects the sample. The intent was to include academic library directors from baccalaureate-, master's-, and doctoral-granting institutions, both public and private. The 17 individuals selected are leaders in the profession, active beyond their local institutions. There was an attempt to achieve gender balance and geographical representation. The purpose of the study is to focus on senior library leaders who are able to reflect knowingly on the traits associated with EI.

In February 2007, those directors received an e-mail questionnaire that identifies four domains (self-awareness, social awareness, self-management, and relationship management) and their associated traits. They were asked to select five traits from each domain that they consider the most important to possess and to rank them in order of their importance from one (highest) to five (lowest).

Fourteen of the 17 leaders participated, a response rate of 82.3 percent. With a larger sample, the rating of traits might differ. Further, because the list of traits per domain is extensive and includes a number of different traits, respondents might have some difficult in making selections and seeing commonalities among all of the traits listed for a domain.[10] Nonetheless, instead of focusing too much on a presentation of findings, this chapter reviews list of traits for emotional intelligence, gathers perceptions about individual ones, and compares the list of traits for EI to a depiction of traits for distributed leadership. At the same time, it offers insights into whether research into distributed leadership should continue and perhaps receive as much attention as EI. The goal is to produce two lists—ones for EI and the other for the distributed model—that individual libraries and leaders can use as a basis for review and mentoring.

Findings

For *self-awareness* (see Table 4.1a), the respondents selected 21 of the 26 traits listed. Nobody added any additional traits. The most frequently checked trait, and one with a low mean score, is "realistic understanding of oneself: emotions, strengths, weaknesses, needs, and drives," which has a mean of 2.00. Seven respondents chose the "ability to listen and delegate" and six favored "cognitive ability to deal with complex scenarios or situations," which has a low mean score. This means that when the directors selected it they were most likely to rate it most important. Another six directors selected "knows where he or she is going—taking the organization," but it had a higher mean score. Among the remaining traits, five directors were most likely to identify:

- Recognize how one's feelings affect others and one's job performance (mean, 3.00)
- Respect individually and diversity (mean, 3.80)
- Sense of humor (mean, 4.20)

To view the above traits from a different perspective, "cognitive ability to deal with complex scenarios or situations" has the lowest mean score, followed by "realistic understanding of oneself: emotions, strengths, weakness needs, and drives" and "ability to listen and delegate."

Turning to *social awareness* (Table 4.1b), the respondents selected 19 of the 22 traits listed. Nobody added any additional traits. No trait stands out as on the previous chart. The trait listed most often is "being open-minded." Viewed from another perspective, of the four traits selected at least five times, "having integrity" has the lowest mean score (mean, 1.80) followed by "attracts, builds, and retains talent" (mean, 2.80), "being open-minded" (mean, 2.86), and "comfortable with team or group culture" (mean, 3.00).

The third chart in the table covers *self-management*. Twenty-six of the 30 traits were selected at least once, and one director added a trait, "effective at keeping up with one's own profession and key peripheral fields." Only three traits were selected at least five times: "integrity" (mean, 2.00), "commitment to job, organization, institution, and profession" (mean, 3.20), and "comfortable with ambiguity" (mean, 3.33).

The final chart addresses *relationship management*. Twenty-two of the 27 traits were selected at least once, and one director added "understands how higher education organizations function and how to get things done within this framework." Five traits were selected at least five times:

Table 4.1
Emotional Intelligence*

A. Self-awareness

Individual Traits	Mean	Respondents (#)
Ability to listen and delegate	2.71	7
Ability to hone one's ability	–	–
Absence of ego (or ego is not a barrier)	5.00	1
Articulate	3.33	3
Assertive	4.00	1
Challenges assumptions	2.00	2
Cognitive ability to deal with complex scenarios or situations	1.67	6
Drive for continual self-improvement at a holistic level	3.50	2
Drive for task completion	1.67	3
Enthusiastic	2.50	4
Intuition	4.50	2
Knows where he or she is going—taking the organization	3.17	6
Narcissism (an acceptable level)	–	–
Realistic understanding of oneself: emotions, strengths, weakness needs, and drives	2.00	10
Recognize how one's feelings affect others and one's job performance	3.00	5
Record of proven leadership	3.00	1
Resilient	5.00	1
Respect individuality and diversity	3.80	5
Respect scholarship, learning, and teaching	3.00	2
Self-confident	4.00	1
Sense of humor	4.20	5
Sense of personal identity	4.00	1
Shows initiative	3.67	3
Spiritual integrity and humility	–	–
Tenacity	–	–
Willingness to tolerate frustration and delay	–	–
Other attributes to add:	–	–

B. Social Awareness

Individual Traits	Mean	Respondents (#)
Ability to understand, anticipate, and harness native behaviors or approaches of staff	2.33	3
Accessible to others	3.00	3
Attracts, builds, and retains talent	2.80	5
Being open-minded	2.86	7
Comfortable with team or group culture	3.00	5
Creates an environment that fosters accountability	2.00	1

Table 4.1
Emotional Intelligence* (continued)

B. Social Awareness (continued)

Individual Traits	Mean	Respondents (#)
Cross-cultural sensitivity and record of achievement	4.50	2
Empathy	2.00	2
Exercises good judgment	3.25	4
Figures out what is going on without having to be told	5.00	1
Genuine belief in the abilities of, and the good faith of, others in the organization	2.40	5
Gives praise generously	–	–
Good interpersonal/people skills	3.67	6
Good listening skills	3.75	4
Having integrity	1.80	5
Interested in others	–	–
Keeps organization focused on high-quality service	3.00	5
Thoughtfully considers the feelings of others	–	–
Treats others as equals	2.00	1
Treats people with dignity/respect	2.50	6
Understands small group dynamics	3.50	2
Wide range of work experiences in different sizes of organizations and different job levels	4.00	2
Other attributes to add:	–	–

C. Self-management

Individual Traits	Mean	Respondents (#)
Ability to compromise	2.67	3
Articulates direction for the library	1.00	3
Asks the "right"/"tough" questions	–	–
Being open-minded	5.00	1
Broad knowledge of issues	3.50	2
Comfortable with ambiguity	3.33	6
Comfortable in making judgment calls	3.67	3
Comfortable with change	3.25	4
Commitment to job, organization, institution, and profession	3.20	5
Courage of convictions	–	–
Diplomatic	3.00	1
Driven to achieve beyond expectations—motivation	2.50	2
Endurance	–	–
Even-handed	–	–
Flexible in adapting to change or overcoming obstacles	2.00	4
Good oral and written presentation skills	5.00	1
Handles stress well	–	–

Table 4.1
Emotional Intelligence* (continued)

C. Self-management (continued)

Individual Traits	Mean	Respondents (#)
High energy level	3.50	2
Honesty	3.50	4
Initiative	4.00	1
Innovative, creative, seeks out and acts on challenges and new opportunities, thinks outside the box	4.50	2
Integrity	2.00	6
Optimism (even in the face of failure)	2.75	4
Propensity for reflection	5.00	1
Realistic organizational awareness	3.67	3
Receptivity to change	3.00	1
Sense of perspective	2.00	3
Skill at diagnostic, strategic, and tactical reasoning	4.00	2
Stable temperament and ability to maintain an emotional balance under constant tensions	2.00	3
Trustworthy	2.00	2
Other attributes to add: Effective at keeping up with one's own profession and key peripheral fields	5.00	1

D. Relationship Management

Individual Traits	Mean	Respondents (#)
Ability to function in a political environment	2.33	3
Ability to gather outside resources	4.00	1
Advocate for librarians' role in higher education	–	–
Brings issues of broad importance to the academic community, fostering wide discussion and action when appropriate	2.75	4
Builds rapport with a wide circle of people	3.00	5
Changes/shapes the library's culture	2.60	5
Collaborative	1.67	3
Consensus building in carrying out strategic direction	2.00	1
Develops and fosters partnerships	2.50	4
Develops staff	4.00	3
Effective in leading change	2.25	4
Enabler and facilitator	3.33	6
Encourages reasonable risk taking	3.00	2
Entrepreneurial	–	–
Establishes credibility with colleagues and stakeholders	3.29	7
Expertise in building and leading teams	1.00	1
Friendly (with a purpose)	1.00	1

Table 4.1
Emotional Intelligence* (continued)

D. Relationship Management (continued)

Individual Traits	Mean	Respondents (#)
Good people networking skills	3.33	3
Helps participants in meetings, consortia, and cooperative endeavors to be results oriented	–	–
Leads in a shared decision-making environment	3.00	2
Mobilizes individual commitment	–	–
Motivates people to develop and adhere to a shared vision	3.00	6
Persuasiveness	–	–
Resonance (inspiring people to work together to solve problems, inspiring excellence)	–	–
Serves as a role model of desired behavior	4.00	1
Tolerates some mistakes	4.00	2
Visionary—able to build a shared vision and rally others around it	3.33	3
Other attributes to add:		
Understands how higher education organizations function and how to get things done within this framework	5.00	1

*The grouped attributes are adapted from Patricia Kreitz, "Leadership and Emotional Intelligence: Study of University Library Directors and Senior Management Teams," unpublished and in-progress study, PhD program in Managerial Leadership in the Information Professions, Simmons College.

- "Changes/shapes the library's culture" (mean, 2.60)
- "Motivates people to develop and adhere to a shared vision" (mean, 3.00)
- "Builds rapport with a wide circle of people" (mean, 3.00)
- "Establishes credibility with colleagues and stakeholders" (mean, 3.29)
- "Enabler and facilitator" (mean, 3.33)

Looking at all of the traits regardless of domain, "realistic understanding of oneself: emotions, strengths, weakness needs, and drives" was selected most often (10 times) and its mean score is 2.00 (*self-awareness*). Next, three traits appear seven times:

- "Ability to listen and delegate" (*self-awareness;* mean, 2.71)
- "Being open-minded" (*social awareness;* mean, 2.86)
- "Establishes credibility with colleagues and stakeholders" (*relationship management;* mean 3.29)

Finally, for the four charts, 20 traits (19% of the 105 traits) were only selected once and 17 (16.2%) went unselected.

EXPLORATION OF THE MODEL
OF DISTRIBUTED LEADERSHIP

As Deborah Ancona, Thomas W. Malone, Wanda J. Orlikowski, and Peter M. Senge comment, there is a myth that leaders are complete—flawless and possessing fully and effectively all of the traits associated with leadership. They also note the importance of senior managers cultivating leadership throughout the organization. Based on a synthesis of their research conducted over a number of years, they advance a model of distributed leadership. That model consists of four interrelated domains or capacities:

1. *sense-making*, defined as "understanding the context in which a company and its people operate"
2. *relating*, defined as "building relationships within and across organizations"
3. *visioning*, defined as "creating a compelling picture of the future"
4. *inventing*, defined as "developing new ways to achieve the vision"[11]

They identify a series of questions that describe each capacity, and it was an easy task to turn those questions into a series of traits. The traits listed for EI were also reviewed to determine if any of them relate to one of the capacities. It merits mention that, because EI provides excellent coverage of visioning, the capacity for visioning includes some of the same traits as found in the list Kreitz produced.

The same directors participating in the study of EI were also asked to select the five most important traits related to the model of distributed leadership and to rank them in order of their preference (from one to five).

Findings

For the category of *sense-making* (Table 4.2a), excluding "creates an environment that fosters accountability," all of the traits were selected at least three times. Four traits were chosen seven times and the mean scores for those range from 2.57 ("recognizes the complexities of many issues") to 4.43 ("open to alternative perspectives and possibilities"). Of the traits mentioned at least six times, one has a mean of 2.00 ("collaborative") and another has a mean of 2.33 ("builds rapport with a wide circle of people").

The next category is *relating*, and one director added "understands what motivates others, particularly subordinates, and how to match responsibilities to fit those motivations." Five of the traits for the category were chosen at least six times. For these traits the mean scores range from 2.17 to 3.00. One trait ("establishes credibility with colleagues and stakeholders") was mentioned nine times and another ("motivates people to develop and adhere to a shared vision") was selected eight times. Another way to view the particular chart is to note that three traits were mentioned twice and another three were chosen three times.

Visioning, the next category, offered the fewest choices. One director added "maintains awareness of a great variety of external factors that could impact libraries and higher education." For the other choices, only "visionary—able to build a shared vision and rally others around it" was not a unanimous selection. For all of the traits listed, "articulates direction for the library" has the lowest mean score, which suggests the overall importance of this trait.

Finally for *inventing,* one trait, "understands small group dynamics," remained unselected, and another one, "drive for task completion," was only selected three times. "Encourages creative ways to solve problems and get work done" was selected the most, and it has the lowest mean score among the traits chosen at least eight times. Of the three traits mentioned 10 times, "resonance (inspiring people to work together to solve problems, inspiring excellence)" has the lowest mean score—2.80.

Looking at the four charts comprising Table 4.2 and the 45 traits listed, only one trait was unselected (2.2%), and 11 (24.4%) were mentioned no more than three times. There was the greatest agreement for *visioning.* The next largest numbers appear for *inventing,* and there was more variation for the remaining two categories: *sense-making* and *relating.* For two categories, *relating* and *visioning,* a trait was added. Perhaps had respondents been aware of them, selections might have varied somewhat.

COMPARISON OF ATTRIBUTES FOR EMOTIONAL INTELLIGENCE AND DISTRIBUTED LEADERSHIP

Because the respondents had an opportunity to reflect on two different models, each approaching leadership from a different perspective, the logical question becomes, "Do they prefer one over the other?" It is clear that not all do; each perspective has its place. Six respondents expressed no preference for one list over the other, four preferred the distributed model, and the remaining three favored emotional intelligence.

The supporters of EI noted that the concept is older, that more attention has focused on it, and that they feel more comfortable describing themselves in terms of the concept. One director commented,

One of the challenges was that the tables for EI [in the questionnaire] were more difficult to complete because there are more traits in each category than there were for the categories in the distributed model. This might make me favor the DM; however, I find the categories of *inventing* and *visioning* narrower pieces of the total concept than were the four domains of the EI model. So I prefer the EI model.

Another supporter of EI thinks that both models are "related/similar. I am something of an intuitive type manager. I don't manage in a hands-on fashion, but rely on others. I concentrate on vision, relating and inspiring staff, collaboration, etc. EI is very important in my management philosophy."

Table 4.2
Model of Distributed Leadership*

A. Sense-making	Mean	Respondents (#)
Ability to marshal outside resources and support	2.00	3
Build rapport with a wide circle of people	2.33	6
Collaborative	2.00	6
Creates an environment that fosters accountability	5.00	1
Keeps organization focused on high-quality service	3.00	7
Open to alternative perspectives and possibilities	4.43	7
Realistic organizational awareness	4.00	5
Receptive to change	3.75	4
Recognizes the complexities of many issues	2.57	7
Seeks different perspectives	3.20	5
Sense of perspective	2.50	4
Skilled at diagnostic, strategic, and tactical reasoning	2.86	7
Willingness to test observations and assumptions	3.00	3
Other attributes to add:	–	–

B. Relating	Mean	Respondents (#)
Anticipates how others will react to his/her ideas	4.50	2
Being open-minded	2.83	6
Develops and fosters partnerships	2.17	6
Encourages others to express their views	3.67	3
Establishes credibility with colleagues and stakeholders	2.44	9
Explains his/her ideas well	2.00	2
Exercises good judgment	3.00	5
Explains the reasoning process (behind his/her ideas)	3.00	2
Good interpersonal/people skills	4.00	4
Good listening skills	4.00	3
Good oral and written communication skills	5.00	2
Innovative, creative, seeks out and acts on challenges and new opportunities, and thinks outside the box	2.00	4
Leads in a shared decision-making environment	2.67	3
Motivates people to develop and adhere to a shared vision	2.75	8
Relates well to others when giving/receiving advice, when seeking help, or thinking through difficult problems	3.25	4
Understands the perspectives of others	3.00	6
Other attributes to add:		
Understands what motivates others, particularly subordinates, and how to match responsibilities to fit those motivations	4.00	1

C. Visioning	Mean	Respondents (#)
Articulates direction for the library	2.21	14
Changes/shapes the library's culture	3.00	14

Table 4.2
Model of Distributed Leadership* (continued)

C. Visioning (continued)	*Mean*	*Respondents (#)*
Comfortable with change	3.43	14
Knows where he or she is going—taking the organization	3.57	14
Visionary—able to build a shared vision and rally others around it	2.61	13
Other attributes to add:		
Maintains awareness of a great variety of external factors that could impact libraries and higher education	5.00	1

D. Inventing	*Mean*	*Respondents (#)*
Challenges assumptions	3.00	10
Cognitive ability to deal with complex scenarios or situations	2.75	8
Comfortable with team culture	3.00	8
Drive for task completion	1.67	3
Encourages creative ways to solve problems and get work done	2.45	11
Expertise in building and leading teams	3.00	1
Flexible in grouping and linking people	3.89	10
Resonance (inspiring people to work together to solve problems, inspiring excellence)	2.80	10
Understands small group dynamics	–	–
Willing to consider other ways to get work done	3.44	9
Other attributes to add:	–	–

*See Deborah Ancona, Thomas W. Malone, Wanda J. Orlikowski, and Peter M. Senge, "In Praise of the Incomplete Leader," *Harvard Business Review* 85, no. 2 (February 2007): 92–100.

One of the directors favoring the distributed model thinks that EI has "multiple ways to express the same idea. For example, integrity, honesty, and trustworthiness appear to me to be facets of the same trait. Was I to mark them all? Or to choose one, as I did." Another director favors the distributed model because it contains fewer traits and "seems more focused on the skills that are associated with leadership. However, it seems odd that 'innovative, creating' was under *relating* rather than *inventing*." Two directors mentioned that the distributed model resonated with them:

- "It is a clear and relatively simple conceptual framework that rings true, based upon my observations and knowledge of senior and middle level college administrators. Individual administrators or managers with strength in one area can get into unnecessary difficulty when they do not consult with others, test their assumptions, or do not compensate for their weaknesses."

- "The groupings seem more closely related to the way skills cluster in actual leadership situations. The 'emotional intelligence' charts [see Table 4.1] lump a lot of characteristics under such broad areas that it is hard to say what those areas actually mean. (There is not enough differentiation, perhaps, because each seems so comprehensive.)"

CONCLUSION

Both leadership theories and styles have their place. No single set of traits applies to every leadership situation, and it is unlikely that anybody possesses all of the traits that characterize any particular leadership style. As Bill George, Peter Sims, Andrew N. McLean, and Diana Mayer note, there is no "cookie-cutter leadership style" and "no one can be authentic by trying to imitate someone else."[12] As a consequence, there is little need to continue to refine or perfect a list of traits that might have universal application or that might make individuals a replica of someone else. Instead, organizations and their leaders should select the subset of traits related to emotional intelligence, the distributed model of leadership, or some other style that is most relevant to their situation. Any subset can then be easily converted into a 360-degree assessment form and thereby be useful to any organization and its leaders as they continue to develop their abilities and skills.[13]

"Modern organizations are far too complex to be transformed by a single giant."[14]

NOTES

1. Deborah Ancona and others, "In Praise of the Incomplete Leader," *Harvard Business Review* 85, no. 1 (February 2007): 92.

2. David R. Caruso, "MSCEIT: Mayer-Salovey-Caruso Emotional Intelligence Test Resource Report," Multi-Health Systems Inc, 2004, 2–4, http://www.mhs.com/ROE/MSCEITResource.pdf (accessed January 4, 2007).

3. The EQ Store, "Assessment: Mayer-Salovey-Caruso Emotional Intelligence Test + Debrief 87," http://www.6seconds.org/xcart/product.php?productid = 87 (accessed January 4, 2007).

4. For "Example MSCEIT [Test] Items," see the Web site maintained by David Caruso, http://www.emotionaliq.org/MSCEITExamples.htm (accessed January 4, 2006).

5. John D. Mayer, "What Is Emotional Intelligence (EI)? How Does This Model Compare to Other Approaches to Emotional Intelligence?" http://www.unh.edu/emotional_intelligence/index.html (accessed January 4, 2006). This source expands on the advantages of this particular model.

6. Peter Hernon and Nancy Rossiter, "Emotional Intelligence: Which Traits Are Most Prized?" *College & Research Libraries* 67, no. 3 (May 2006): 260–75.

7. Ibid., 271.

8. Patricia Kreitz, "Leadership and Emotional Intelligence: Study of University Library Directors and Senior Management Teams" (unpublished and in-progress study, PhD program in managerial leadership in the information professions, Simmons College).

9. Ancona and others, "In Praise of the Incomplete Leader," 92, 100.

10. It merits mention that only one director mentioned this as a problem.

11. Ancona and others, "In Praise of the Incomplete Leader," 94.

12. Bill George and others, "Discovering Your Authentic Leadership," *Harvard Business Review* 85, no. 2 (February 2007): 129.

13. Peter Hernon and Nancy Rossiter, *Making a Difference: Leadership and Academic Libraries* (Westport, CT: Libraries Unlimited, 2007), chap. 15.

14. The CEO Refresher, "Leading Change" (views of John P. Kotter), http://www.refresher.com/!leading (accessed February 7, 2007).

5

TRACES OF ACADEMIC LIBRARY LEADERSHIP

Peter Hernon

"Leadership is a complex social phenomenon."[1]

In a search for new and more meaningful ways to study leadership, researchers in various disciplines and professions have relied on different theoretical frameworks (e.g., constructive-developmental theory, which "is a stage theory of adult development that focuses on the growth and elaboration of a person's way of understanding the self and the world");[2] quantitative and qualitative research designs,[3] with the case study perhaps being the most common; and different methods of data collection, including survey research, the use of standardized tests (e.g., the Mayer-Salovey-Caruso Emotional Intelligence Test), panel reviews (for the development of leadership accountability scales),[4] and observation. Survey research encompasses the use of questionnaires, focus group interviews, interviews (perhaps semi-structured ones), and occasionally diaries, which are "a kind of self-administered questionnaire."[5]

Using semi-structured interviews, one study linked leadership development to succession planning in 15 best-practice organizations. These organizations used managerial personnel to develop a mentor network, identify and codify "high potential employees," establish "a flexible and fluid succession planning process," create "organization-wide forums for exposing high potential employees to multiple stakeholders," and develop "a supportive organizational culture." The premise of the study is that

organizations of all sizes and industries are currently facing a range of leadership development challenges, including mid-management levels that often rob high-potential managers of critical on-the-job experiences, depleted resources for employee development,

[and] a rapidly aging workforce that may create shortfalls of experienced managerial talent for senior leadership positions.[6]

Given the vast body of research on leadership, there is an occasional meta-analysis, a technique of synthesizing findings by using statistical methods to combine results from separate but related studies and to examine underlying assumptions.[7] Thierry C. Pauchant proposes including three methodologies to examine leadership: interpretative biography, which provides an account of someone's life and shows how that person attributes subjective meaning to his or her inner experiences; institutional analysis, which emphasizes organizations in their relationships with a broader environment; and historical inquiry, which examines the macro-context of organizations and relates it to social systems and individuals.[8]

Peter C. Gronn and Peter Ribbins advocate using ethnography and biography to research leadership. "An ethnographic approach to leadership aims to determine the understanding that leaders have of their leadership and the factors that influence that understanding," and a biography facilitates "theorizing about leadership in that...[it offers] proof of the development and learning of leadership attributes, provide[s] information on the ends to which leaders have directed their attitudes, and answer[s] institutional-level questions."[9]

Qualitative research might rely on grounded theory, which "is a method for discovering theories, concepts, hypotheses, and propositions directly from data, rather than from a priori assumptions, other research, or existing theoretical frameworks."[10] As C. Lakshman notes, "the end result is theory, which needs to be tested and refined through other conventional mechanisms."[11]

The research does not necessarily focus on leaders themselves. It might examine how leadership happens and what results occur. In such instances, leadership might be blended with management and greater effort centers on how managerial leaders function as organizations transform. The following study applies content analysis to examine a set of documents that blend management and leadership within academic librarianship. Content analysis "has potential for leadership research, but a drawback is that the richness of qualitative data may be lost." However, studies like the one conducted by Chao C. Chen and James R. Meindl show the potential of content analysis.[12]

A STUDY OF "EXCELLENT" LIBRARIES

Beginning with 2000, Blackwell's Book Services has provided the Association of College and Research Libraries (ACRL), American Library Association, with "funding for an Excellence in Academic Libraries Award Program to recognize an outstanding community college, college, and university library each year. This award...[recognizes] the accomplishments of librarians and other library staff as they come together as members of a team to support the mission of their institution. Blackwell's gift of $12,000 provides a $3,000 gift to each of the three winning libraries and $3,000 to support travel by an ACRL officer to the three award ceremonies."[13]

According to Larry Hardesty,

The winning libraries usually receive the award because of a multiplicity of efforts often sustained over an extended period of time. These efforts typically reflect:

- ready adoption and creative use of technology
- development of the library as "the place" for communication and collaboration among users
- clear sense of service and dedication among the library staff in both anticipating and responding to individual user needs through personal attention[14]

As a consequence, these libraries "should serve as inspiration to other libraries."[15]

From 2000 through 2007, 23 libraries received the award. Seven of them are affiliated with community colleges, eight with colleges, and the remaining eight with universities. The universities are predominately members of the Association of Research Libraries. The applications of the winning libraries, which are available online, were examined for references to leadership traits and competencies as defined through the models discussed in the previous chapter as well as the leadership model that characterizes the PhD Program in Managerial Leadership at the Graduate School of Library and Information Science, Simmons College.[16]

Findings of Content Analysis

Colleges and Community Colleges

The applications for these libraries equate leadership with accomplishments, reflect how organizations are engaged in managing change, and view results in a team context. That context, however, cannot be linked to a particular leadership theory such as transformational leadership. Further, the references to leadership are general and make it difficult to distinguish between leadership and effective management, which is results oriented. There are discussions about creating new services and improving existing ones, engaging the campus community, providing services beyond the local institution, staff development, and making organizations more efficient.

The applications identify numerous input and output metrics, and there is occasional mention of outcomes, which is defined in terms of accomplishments or changes resulting from exposure to information literacy. Discussions of "leadership in the profession" tend to reflect what different staff members did; more specifically, what they wrote, what conferences they attended, and so on. There was no indication about how such activities comprise leadership.

The specific references to leadership mention "forward-thinking leadership," "productive partnerships," "productive relationships," collaboration with other academic departments, "intense collaboration," "creativity and innovation," and "lead partner in an innovative collaboration." They detail a leadership role "in making e-textbooks available" to students, in participating in networks, in "Web page development," in "promoting technology-based information competency," and "in consortial purchase negotiations," but the applications do not elaborate on the leadership component. An indicator of leadership might relate to the prior receipt of national awards:

Richland College Library received the EBSCO Award for Program Achievement (presented by the Community and Junior College Library Section of the Association of College and Research Libraries), and in 2001, the library received the ALA/Information Today Library of the Future Award. The Richland College Library was the first community college library in the United States to receive this award. Both of these awards were for the library's proactive information literacy program.

Other direct indicators of leadership are receipt of a national leadership grant from the Institute of Museum and Library Services (IMLS) and mention by regional accreditation organizations such as the Middle States Commission on Higher Education (MSCHE) of the role that the library plays within the institution. For example,

- The 2000 MSCHE Evaluation Team noted that "the library administration provides strong internal planning and organizational leadership. Outwardly, the library administration is active on College-wide committees, and works collaboratively with academic departments in the use of instructional technologies" (Baruch College).
- "The Middle States review and the accreditation standards presented a golden opportunity to advocate for the library as an academic department and put forward a new, more dynamic image of library faculty—that of educator and faculty partner. We did this by identifying the most important initiatives on our campus and worked to demonstrate how the library department supports those initiatives. In our case these priorities were retention, recruitment, academic integrity, and writing across the curriculum" (Eugenio María de Hostos Community College).
- The report of the visit conducted by the North Central Commission on Accreditation and School Improvement was used as evidence supporting the content of the application. The library also showed how it had responded to concerns raised by the assessment team. For example, "the Report points to the centrality of the library to the Earlham community and comments positively on the bibliographic instruction program and the newly renovated building. The Report also commented on future plans and concerns. I am pleased to report that we have acted favorably on all of the Report's comments" (Earlham College).
- During the past four years library faculty have been active in the College's Student Outcomes Assessment program since the formation of a college-wide assessment

committee. A librarian serves as editor for *re:Assessment,* the official committee newsletter distributed to all faculty and administrators (College of DuPage).

The Pierce College Library devotes a section of its application to "leadership in assessment" and being "one of the first colleges to adopt Information Competency outcomes." There is, however, no clarification about the type of outcome. The application also mentions that:

- "Each library faculty member incorporates assessment into library instruction sessions based on these Information Competency outcomes. In addition, all library departments have developed outcomes, indicators, assessments, and criteria for their work. . . . The Library undertook the project because we feel everyone in the library, regardless of position or role, contributes to student success."
- "Outcomes and assessments were collaboratively developed from 2001 to 2003, and assessments began in 2003. Each department has designed both strategic (long-term) outcomes, as well as annual outcomes that are geared toward immediate improvement. The library budget is integrated into the process and developed based on what is identified in the assessments. In addition to productivity outcomes, each department has outcomes pertaining to its role in student success and communication with other units."

The Anne Arundel Community College Library views itself as a trendsetter as, according to its application, it "was the first Maryland community college to provide a separate library web page specifically for distance learners." Its application also discusses building partnership with teaching faculty and the development of "college-wide information literacy outcomes." Further, there are sections on statewide and campus-wide leadership as well as on:

- "Involvement in accreditation standards. The previous library director was a member of the Task Force on Learning and Teaching, a Middle States Association task group that rewrote accreditation standards. The current library director is a member of the ACRL/Community and Junior College Libraries Section Standards Committee, which is revising the guidelines for 2-year college libraries and learning resources centers and she is also chairing the college's self-study process that will result in a consideration for reaccreditation by the Middle States Association in spring 2004."

Universities

Similar to the applications for the colleges and community colleges, the eight applications for university libraries focus on accomplishments and the provision of a wide set of services for their local communities as well as engagement at the national level. There is also coverage of effective management revolving around the setting and accomplishment of a strategic plan, the creation of an organizational structure that supports library initiatives and goals, the movement from a hierarchical to a flattened organization, the development of new services and facilities, and the possession of a productive staff.[17] There is mention of libraries reinventing and transforming themselves, actively engaged in change management, garnering campus acclaim, and registering a national impact.

As for specific indicators of leadership, the applications refer to listening to faculty and students; acting on what they say; creating partnerships and being collaborative internal and external to the institution (e.g., with consortia); gaining campus support to take certain actions on scholarly communications; and being creative, forward thinking, and innovative. Activities such as involvement in library and other committees, as well as engaging in staff development, may involve leadership; however, that connection is not explained. In its application, Loyola University New Orleans mentions the library "has become more flexible and provides opportunities for leadership at all levels of faculty and staff," but does not elaborate.

The application for The Georgia Institute of Technology Library and Information Center notes,

As the Library pursues its ambitious agenda, a new organizational culture is emerging. We are [moving] away from planning and directive from the top down and towards engaging staff at all levels to our work. Recommendations for change are consistently tested against the question, "How does suggestion improve the academic welfare, support and success of students and faculty?" We focus [on] giving staff the necessary skills to succeed at their work. Many jobs have been re-engineered in a changing work environment to improve efficiencies in work-flow and to facilitate the emphasis digital agenda. Significantly more funds are directed to staff training, technical certification and participation in conferences. Comprehensive salary reviews with market comparisons have resulted [in] significant salary increases throughout the organization, facilitated by strong support from University administration. This cultural shift improves the recruitment and retention of talented staff.

A direct indication of leadership is, "Individuals from all levels of the organization are encouraged to participate in committees and working groups that previously relied on librarians. Creativity and risk-taking are endorsed to accelerate the flow of ideas and encourage experimentation. Individuals are given time and resources to develop and implement promising ideas." One of those ideas is a conference that a team of libraries across the nation put together.

As part of its culture of assessment, the University of Washington mentions collaboration "with related campus groups to include survey questions of mutual interest (especially information technology and student learning) on the triennial surveys, in addition to library-related questions on surveys run by other campus agencies." Further, "The Libraries' assessment efforts and ability to use the results to improve library services were recognized in the 2003 decennial accreditation review of the University."

"Through a partnership with the Office of Undergraduate Education and Computing & Communications, the University Libraries created UWired...[,] a forum for promoting broad-based discussions, experimentation and analysis about innovation in teaching and learning with technology, fluency in information technology, and new ways for students and faculty to access technology tools and resources." Recognition of UWired's leadership role comes from receipt of the ACRL Innovation in Instruction Award in 1995 and the national EDUCAUSE Award for Systemic Progress in Teaching and Learning in 2000.

Educating the faculty about scholarly communication and seeing this effort result in the Faculty Council on University Libraries choosing

scholarly communications as its ongoing agenda in 2001–2003. A UW faculty member, and Nobel Laureate, joined others in founding the Public Library of Science open access initiative. Each of the first two issues of PLoS Biology has featured an article by a UW faculty member. Over 60 faculty signed an open letter calling on scientific publishers to make primary research articles that they publish available online through such initiatives as PubMed Central. The Department of Medical Education and Biomedical Information joined the Libraries in funding the BioMed Central membership. Numerous faculty have chosen to publish through BioMed Central rather than through more expensive journals.

The Libraries claims it "is an acknowledged leader in campus diversity issues," as well as "nationally recognized for programs of excellence in library assessment, information literacy, digital libraries, international studies support, integrated health information services, and for providing access to networked information. The Libraries is also known for its commitment to collaborative programs to facilitate teaching and learning."

Loyola University New Orleans notes that "the provost has recognized the library as a model learning organization on campus. She sees the library leading the rest of the university in terms of its non-hierarchical organizational structure." Further, "the library is recognized as a leader on campus for instruction in information and instructional technology applications for research and teaching. One result of the library's good reputation in instructional technology was the invitation to become the instructional team for the campus adoption of Blackboard courseware."

The application of Cornell University Library (CUL) mentions its leadership "in digital library research and implementation for over a decade" and in teaching information literacy, and it refers to the accreditation report of the MSCHE: "We take pride in the finding of the MSA/CHE [Council on Higher Education] evaluation team that CUL is 'a leader and pacesetter among North American libraries, recognized for its large and rich collections, its knowledgeable and service-oriented staff, its rich array of user-based programs, and its digital library gateway, access structure, and rich content of knowledge and information resources.'"

This application was the only one to mention lobbying and being successful with it: "the Library successfully lobbied against the fee-for-service model as an impairment of open access to valuable information resources."

The application of the University of Arizona Library refers to cooperative projects with faculty members. For example, the library is co-publisher of an electronic journal with an entomology professor. "Begun with a subsidy from the Library, it will be supported in the long term by partnerships the Library will develop with other academic institutions."

Finally, the application of North Carolina State University Libraries refers to the library as "an early leader in establishing a flexible network infrastructure that gives our users exceptionally powerful, very high bandwidth access to digital resources." The application also demonstrates library success in the political arena, when the library was recipient of "an unprecedented 35% increase in our annual state-appropriated budget."

General Impressions

The 23 applications provide a general overview of the libraries receiving the award and suggest that they are actively engaged in evidence-based decision making, that is, the collection of data to guide decisions and planning. The different staffs actively engage in the conduct of survey research and some rely on usability studies for formative evaluation, the purpose of which seems to be to improve the delivery of Web-based services.

Table 5.1 takes the leadership theories discussed in the previous chapter (see tables 4.1 and 4.2), as well as the leadership model guiding the doctoral program at the Graduate School of Library and Information Science, Simmons College, and attempts to identify the traits and competencies covered in the various applications. Without a formal on-campus review of each library, the list is merely suggestive. Some of the traits and competencies (e.g., "drive for task completion") are implicit given the range of accomplishments listed. The tables in the previous chapter mention accountability; the applications focus on evidence-based decision making but raise accountability in the context of the regional accrediting organizations.

The Simmons model, which is derived from the National Center for Healthcare Leadership, focuses on three broad areas:

- Transformation: visioning, energizing, and stimulating a change process that coalesces communities, patrons, and professionals around new models of managerial leadership.

- Accomplishment: translating vision and strategy into optimal organizational performance.

- People: creating an organizational climate that values employees from all backgrounds and provides an energizing environment for them. It also includes the leader's responsibility to understand his or her impact on others and to improve his or her capabilities, as well as the capabilities of others.

Table 5.1
Leadership Traits Covered in the Applications

Emotional Intelligence	Model of Distributed Leadership	Simmons Leadership Model
Self-awareness Drive for task completion Knows where he or she is going—taking the organization Respect scholarship, learning, and teaching	**Sense-making** Ability to function in a political environment Ability to marshal outside resources and support Build rapport with a wide circle of people Collaborative Creates an environment that fosters accountability Keeps organization focused on high-quality service Receptive to change	**Transformation** Achievement orientation Community orientation Innovative thinking
Social-awareness Comfortable with team and group culture Creates an environment that fosters accountability Good listening skills Keeps organization focused on high-quality service		**Accomplishment** Organizational awareness Accountability Change leadership Collaboration Information technology management initiative
Self-management Articulates direction for the library Comfortable with change Innovative, creative, seeks out and acts on challenges and new opportunities, thinks outside the box	**Relating** Develops and fosters partnerships Establishes credibility with colleagues and stakeholders Good listening skills Innovative, creative, seeks out and acts on challenges and new opportunities, thinks outside the box	**People** Relationship-building
Relationship Management Ability to gather outside resources Builds rapport with a wide circle of people Changes/shapes the library's culture Collaborative Develops and fosters partnerships Develops staff Effective in leading change Helps participants in meetings, consortia, and cooperative endeavors to be results-oriented	**Visioning** Articulates direction for the library Changes/shapes the library's culture **Inventing** Comfortable with team culture	

The competencies covering *transformation* include:

- Achievement orientation: a concern for surpassing a standard of excellence. The standard may be one's own past performance (striving for improvement); an objective measure (results orientation); outperforming others (competitiveness); challenging goals, or something that has been done previously (innovation).

- Community orientation: the ability to align one's own and the organization's priorities with the needs and values of the community, including its cultural and ethnocentric values, and to move managerial leadership forward. It includes a service orientation to both external and internal "customers" and constituencies.

- Innovative thinking: the ability to apply complex concepts, develop creative solutions, or adapt.

The competencies for *accomplishment* are:

- Communication skills: the ability to speak and write in a clear, logical, and grammatical manner in formal and informal situations; to prepare cogent business presentations; and to facilitate a group. It is also the ability to persuade, convince, influence, or impress others (individuals or groups) in order to get them to go along with or to support one's opinion or position.

- Accountability: the ability to hold people accountable to standards of performance or ensure compliance using the power of one's position or force of personality appropriately and effectively, with the long-term good of the organization in mind. This includes involving people in developing the standards that impact their performance measurement.

- Change leadership: the ability to energize stakeholders and sustain their commitment to changes in approaches, processes, and strategies.

- Collaboration: the ability to work cooperatively with others, to be part of a team, to work together, as opposed to working separately or competitively. Collaboration applies when a person is a member of a group of people functioning as a team, but is not the leader.

- Information technology management initiative: the ability to see the potential in, understand, and use administrative information tools, including active sponsorship of system use and the continuous upgrading of information management capabilities. The ability to make decisions and solve problems proactively—to identify a problem, obstacle, or opportunity and take action in light of this identification to address current or future problems or opportunities. In this context, initiative also includes the ability to involve staff or other stakeholders in the decision-making and problem-solving processes to ensure greater cooperation and accountability among those implementing or affected by the decision or solution.

Only one competency, relationship building, emerges for the leadership area of *people*. It is defined as "the ability to establish, build and sustain professional contacts for the purpose of building networks of people with similar goals and that support similar interests."

Findings of Home Page Analysis

The home pages of the 23 libraries were examined for information that might supplement the coverage of leadership in the previous section of the chapter. None of the resources reviewed added traits and competencies to table 5.1. Especially for the early award winners, new services might be identified in the planning documents found on the home pages.

A Case Study

Given the convenient location of Wellesley College, an award winner, to one of the authors, the library was selected for a site visit, the purpose of which was to probe the topic of leadership. In the 1990s, the library merged with information technology and the library regrouped as Information Services. The regrouping involved an intensive review of services, organizational structures, and workflow patterns. The review process centered on the development of a shared vision to guide the library for the future. A key expectation was that the library professional and support staff would be empowered and committed to thinking about the future and providing high-quality service. As a result of that review, the managerial hierarchy was flattened, thereby reducing the vertical reporting structure and encouraging staff to work together collaboratively.

The college supports a collaborative model of leadership and wants staff, those in managerial and non-managerial roles, to accept leadership roles. Toward this end, the Department of Human Resources engaged in a six-month review of the roles and responsibilities of staff around campus. That review resulted in the adoption of a set of criteria for evaluating staff performance and rewarding staff—supporting their continued development. The chapter appendix explains the different criteria, several of which include aspects of leadership.

As part of their annual development plan, which identifies their major activities for the year, individual staff members identify which criteria they will address. For instance, to accomplish a particular activity, they might seek to inspire or mentor others. Some staff members in non-managerial positions are actively engaged in data collection (e.g., through the use of focus group interviews) that applies to the library's mission and current planning efforts. Such efforts illustrate that the staff go beyond task completion and are engaged in activities that impact the college and the library, as well as shaping a changing work environment.

From the interview, it is evident that library staff think strategically about the place of the library within the institution. The emphasis is on working collaboratively and producing results beneficial to the institution and the individual. Within such a context, the reasons that the library received the award become evident.

Further Research

All of the recipients of the award might comprise a study population to gather more detailed insights into academic library leadership. Individual leaders, be they the directors or other staff members, might be matched against particular leadership styles and the set of traits and competencies highlighted in the previous chapter. The distributed model and the Simmons leadership model go beyond individual traits and afford more opportunities to focus on leadership within the libraries, thereby better distinguishing between management and leadership. Such research might also examine the evolution of these libraries into nationally acclaimed, "excellent" libraries and reveal how the staff work together to accomplish a shared vision and the institutional mission.

CONCLUSION

A close examination of the applications of the 23 award winners suggests that the documents focus mostly on management and do not fully explain the leadership component. The assumption might be that any significant accomplishments would not have occurred without the presence of leadership, perhaps throughout the organization. As numerous scholars and other authors have noted, however, leadership and management are not synonymous.[18] Leaders take charge, energize and motivate followers, set new directions, and translate a shared vision into reality. Managers focus on efficiency and execute or implement existing directions, whereas managerial leaders are transformational.

"Yet while much has been written about character traits and issues of openness and trust, the leadership literature has had strikingly little to say about what a leader should be able to expect from his people."[19]

NOTES

1. Cynthia D. McCauley and others, "The Use of Constructive-Development Theory to Advance the Understanding of Leadership," *The Leadership Quarterly* 17 (2006): 650.

2. Ibid.

3. See, for instance, Alan Bryman, "Qualitative Research on Leadership: A Critical but Appreciative Review," *Leadership Quarterly* 15, no. 6 (2004): 729–69; Jay A. Conger, "Qualitative Research as the Cornerstone Methodology for Understanding Leadership," *Leadership Quarterly* 9, no. 1 (1998): 107–21; Susan R. Madsen, "Developing Leadership: Exploring Childhoods of Women University Presidents," *Journal of Educational Administration* 45, no. 1 (2007): 99–118.

4. James A. Wood and Bruce E. Winston, "Development of Three Scales to Measure Leader Accountability," *Leadership & Organization Development Journal* 28, no. 2 (2007): 167–85.

5. Colin Robson, *Real World Research: A Resource for Social Scientists and Practitioner-Researchers* (Oxford, U.: Blackwell, 1993), 254.

6. Kevin S. Groves, "Integrating Leadership Development and Succession Planning Best Practices," *Journal of Management Development* 26, no. 3 (2007): 239.

7. See Appa Rao Korukonda and James G. Hunt, "Premises and Paradigms in Leadership Research," *Journal of Organizational Change Management* 4, no. 2 (1991): 19–33.

8. Thierry C. Pauchant, "Integral Leadership: A Research Proposal," *Journal of Organizational Change Management* 18, no. 2 (2005): 211–29.

9. Peter C. Gronn and Peter Ribbins, "Leaders in Context: Postpositivist Approaches to Understanding Educational Leadership," *Educational Administration Quarterly* 32 (1996): 452.

10. Steven Taylor and Robert Bogdan, *Introduction to Qualitative Research Methods,* 2nd ed. (New York: Wiley and Sons, 1984), 126. See also Ken W. Parry, "Grounded Theory and Social Process: A New Direction for Leadership Research," *Leadership Quarterly* 9, no. 1 (1998), 21 pages. Available from *Business Source Premier* (accessed March 14, 2007); Ronald R. Powell and Lynn Silipigni Connaway, *Basic Research Methods for Librarians,* 4th ed. (Westport, CT: Libraries Unlimited, 2004), 201–02.

11. C. Lakshman, "Organizational Knowledge Leadership: A Grounded Theory Approach," *Leadership & Organization Development Journal* 28, no. 1 (2007): 51.

12. Parry, "Grounded Theory and Social Process," 3. See also Chao C. Chen and James R. Meindl, "The Construction of Leadership Images in the Popular Press: The Case of Donald Burr and People Express," *Administrative Science Quarterly* 36, no. 4 (1991): 521–51; David L. Ford Jr., and Kiran M. Ismail, "Perceptions of Effective Leadership among Central Eurasian Managers: A Cultural Convergence-divergence Examination within a Globalization Context," *Journal of International Management* 12, no. 2 (2006): 158–80.

13. American Library Association, Association of College and Research Libraries, "Excellence in Academic Libraries Award," Association of College and Research Libraries, 2007, http://www.ala.org/ala/acrl/acrlawards/excellenceacademic.htm (accessed March 22, 2007).

14. Larry Hardesty, "Excellence in Academic Libraries: Recognizing It," *Library Issues: Briefings for Faculty and Administrators* 27, no. 4 (March 2007): 1, http://0-www.libraryissues.com.library.simmons.edu/ (accessed March 22, 2007).

15. Ibid., 3.

16. Peter Hernon and Nancy Rossiter, *Making a Difference: Leadership and Academic Libraries* (Westport, CT: Libraries Unlimited, 2007), 229–50.

17. The application of Cornell University Library mentions that "the July 1999 issue of *College & Research Libraries* listed the 'Most Productive Libraries 1993–1997,' based on the number of peer-reviewed articles in the professional library literature. CUL was ranked second, with a total of 32 publications with lead authors from Cornell. The library profession and others engaged in digital library research benefit from the research and expertise contributed by the Cornell staff."

18. Warren Bennis, *On Becoming a Leader* (Reading, MA: Addison-Wesley, 1989), 34.

19. Larry Bossidy, "What Your Leader Expects of You and What You Should Expect in Return," *Harvard Business Review* 85, no. 3 (April 2007): 58.

APPENDIX: VALUING WORK @ WELLESLEY: ROLE CLASSIFICATION*

The cornerstone of the Valuing Work @ Wellesley College program is the Role Classification System. Employees, managers, and the senior leadership of the College worked together to create a model for Role Classification that will help Wellesley College effectively meet the challenges of technology, a changing workforce, innovation, and fast-paced change.

Purposes of Role Classification

While there has been a Classification Model at Wellesley for many years, the project team revisited its purpose and desired role before embarking on the design of a new system.

- There is a shift at the College, and in the work world at large, to consider work in terms of a role rather than a job. The increased use of technology and the resulting changes in organizational structure has changed the focus in today's workplace from a collection of tasks to be completed, a job, to the primary responsibilities, performance indicators, and competencies (skills) required for the work, a role. Wellesley's classification system should be based on roles.

- The classification system needs to communicate the types of skills, or competencies, that are required for various roles at the College. Areas of competency must be identified, defined, and described at various levels in order to classify roles meaningfully. In this way, the classification model reinforces an atmosphere of skill-building competencies common to roles across different areas of the College and opportunities for role movement among them.

- An effective classification model will show how each area of skill, or competency, can be demonstrated at various levels, providing a basis for training, career development, and succession planning.

- Finally, Wellesley College has been a successful institution because its values are clear and provide a solid foundation for Wellesley's reputation among institutions of higher education and in the community. It is critical that the classification model be built with these values in mind, so that employees of the College reflect and practice these values in their work, and that these values are in turn built into the performance management and compensation systems.

Changes in Wellesley's Role Classification System: What We Value

The classification model previously used at the College fulfilled some of the purposes described above. Jobs were considered for classification using the following factors:

---

*©Working@Wellesley: An Online Guide to Wellesley College Human Resources. Available at http://www.wellesley.edu/HR/new/VWSite/vwcontents.html (accessed May 7, 2007). Please note that this is an internal document and any use requires permission from the Department of Human Resources, Wellesley College, Wellesley, MA.

- Knowledge
- Experience
- Complexity of decision making
- Impact of decisions
- Internal contacts
- External contacts
- Communications
- Work environment
- Supervisory responsibility
- Number of employees supervised

The current classification model retains some of these factors, while replacing and/or adding others. Roles at Wellesley are now considered for classification using the following factors:

- Service to constituents
- Communication
- Expertise
- Innovation and problem solving, critical thinking
- Accountability/responsibility
- Development of self and others collaboration

The changes in these factors are important to highlight briefly:

- Knowledge and experience is changed to expertise to reflect the collection of skills, education, experience, and functional knowledge required to perform a role.
- Internal and external contacts, impact of decisions, and number of employees supervised was changed to accountability/responsibility to reduce emphasis on one's place in the hierarchical structure or on the relative importance of certain relationships.
- Communication remained a key element of the model but was expanded to include different types of communication responsibilities.
- Perhaps the most noticeable change with the revised model is the factor *service to constituents,* which describes how different roles at Wellesley provide service to various individuals and groups.

After careful consideration, a Valuing Work @ Wellesley design team began to build a model based on the set of seven factors, or areas of competency, listed above. These were seen as being important (in varying degrees) to all types of work at the College. Actual existing roles at the College were used to determine the number of classification levels needed to fully describe all the meaningful gradations of skill/competency for each factor. Each factor is described specifically by use of certain dimensions, or specific competency areas, listed under the factor definitions below.

The Role Classification Factors Defined: What We Value

Service to Constituents

Service to constituents includes the ability to identify, understand, build relationships with, and respond to the needs and expectations of internal and external constituents in an appropriate manner; reflecting the goals and values of the College and demonstrating fiscal responsibility; focusing on the quality and timeliness of constituent programs and services.

Specific dimensions include *constituent knowledge, relationship building,* and *responsiveness and action.*

Expertise

Expertise encompasses the ability to draw upon and utilize specific knowledge, skills and experiences that are needed to perform various Wellesley College roles. Functional knowledge includes both the specialized knowledge pertaining to a specific profession or specialty and knowledge pertaining to general College operations; skills include the ability to utilize technology in response to the changing environment.

Specific dimensions include *functional knowledge and skills,* and e*ducation and experience.*

Accountability / Responsibility

This factor represents the degree to which one is responsible for one's own work, the work of others, and/or delivering services to the Wellesley College community; the impact of a position's end results on the work unit, function or College as a whole and those it serves; the degree of autonomy in decision making required for success; level of review generally given to work process and results; scope of work unit or organization involved.

Specific dimensions include *decision making/impact, role scope/complexity,* and *degree of supervising given/received.*

Collaboration

Collaboration includes the ability to produce successful outcomes by working cooperatively with others; sharing relevant information and soliciting input and assistance of others; integrating input and seeking consensus to reach goals; understanding of team process and problem-solving techniques.

Specific dimensions include *producing results with others* and *collaborating across levels and functions.*

Communication

This factor addresses the ability to effectively interact and exchange information with other members of the Wellesley College community and external constituencies; to develop factual and logical presentations of one's ideas and opinions using written and verbal skills; to demonstrate effective listening skills by shaping and adapting one's own responses to address the issues and styles of others; to demonstrate courtesy and respect and handle confidential information appropriately.

Specific dimensions include w*ritten and verbal, listening and understanding,* and *relating to others.*

Innovation and Problem Solving, Critical Thinking

This factor addresses the ability to identify, define, critically analyze, and resolve work problems through research and testing alternative ideas and approaches; thinking outside traditional parameters, using innovative and creative ideas and actions to improve work processes and service to constituents; seldom settling for a process or service that is "good enough"—adding value and taking measured risks to enhance achievement of the College's mission.

Specific dimensions include p*roblem definition, finding and implementing solutions,* and *ongoing improvement.*

Development of Self and Others

This factor focuses on the practice of providing a strong sense of purpose and mission for the professional development of oneself and others; developing a structure and work process that promotes successful outcomes; serving as an example to others by setting expectations for work, helping each other think through alternatives, and managing diversity; managing one's own development and mentoring/coaching others; seeking appropriate opportunities to expand work-related knowledge, skills, and experiences.

Specific dimensions include *coaching/leading/managing, effecting diversity,* and *career development/training.*

6

EMOTIONAL INTELLIGENCE AND ORGANIZATIONAL AND LEADERSHIP THEORIES

Joan Giesecke

"Clearly work has changed significantly creating new areas for study and a growing need for a conceptual framework for the study of emotions in the workplace."[1]

Organizations are complex social systems that can be viewed from a variety of perspectives. In *Reframing Organizations,* Lee Bolman and Terrence Deal identify four major sets of theories or frames to describe how organizations function. These frames are the structural/rationalist approach, human resources approach, political approach, and symbolic approach.[2] Each frame proposes different approaches for leaders to use to make the organization successful. This section views each frame from the perspective of emotional intelligence to determine the role that EI plays in developing successful approaches for working within these frames.

STRUCTURAL FRAME

The structural frame, based on theories in sociology, emphasizes formal rules and roles. Bureaucratic structures are the most familiar forms of structural approaches to organizations. The rules of the organization determine how decisions are made and who has power in the organization. Problems in the organization are seen as problems of structure and reorganizations are used to resolve systemic problems. Leaders in this environment emphasize implementation of agreed-to projects and goals, using the hierarchy to communicate throughout the organization. EI is not a major factor for those who concentrate on a structural approach to the organization. While poor leaders in this environment can become petty tyrants, they will use rules to enforce their position rather than looking at how personal relationships impact the work place.

HUMAN RESOURCES FRAME

The human resources frame centers on the people in the organization and looks at how people interact. In this approach, developed from the theories of social psychologists, people's feelings, needs, and values are key factors to consider in planning organizational success. Emotional intelligence is a crucial element in the success of leaders working from the human resources perspective. Understanding the emotions of others and learning how to interact effectively are the signs of a successful leader. Failure to understand one's own emotions, the impact one has on others, and others' emotions results in leaders who are ineffective and who will be perceived to have little influence in the organization.

POLITICAL FRAME

In the political frame, organizations are viewed as "arenas in which different interest groups compete for power and scarce resources."[3] People will try to maximize their own goals within the power structure of the organization. Bargaining and negotiating are normal events in the organization. Conflicts arise as individual goals do not mesh with organizational goals. Decisions are the result of successful bargaining behaviors and political skill. Historically, Machiavelli described the skills needed to survive in a highly contentious political environment in his work *The Prince*. His advice is still valuable for today's leaders who find themselves in organizations where the political frame describes the standard operating procedures. In this type of environment, emotional intelligence can be an asset in helping one to understand the other players in the organization. However, manipulative political skills which can be very effective in some organizations are not a part of authentic behaviors associated with high emotional intelligence.

SYMBOLIC FRAME

In the symbolic frame, organizations are viewed as cultures that are propelled by ritual rather than rules.[4] Organizational rituals, myths, and ceremonies are the driving forces in the organization. Leaders in these organizations interpret the environment and actions of others. They set the tone for the organization. They can be very visionary, setting a course for the organization based on high ideals. They work to frame experiences to build on the organizational culture. EI skills are important in the symbolic frame if the leader is to interpret events in ways that touch the emotions of the employees. Leaders need to understand what emotions are present in a situation, how people are feeling about the environment, and then respond in ways that tap into those emotions.

LEARNING ORGANIZATION

Another organizational theory that is useful for leaders to review is that of the learning organization. "A learning organization is an organization skilled at creating, acquiring, and transferring knowledge, and at modifying its behavior to reflect new knowledge and insights. Without accompanying changes in the way that work gets done, only the potential for improvement exists."[5] In a successful learning organization, new knowledge translates into new ways of behaving. Leaders and employees seek new knowledge, share ideas among units, and exchange information throughout the organization, all in an effort to improve the organization and to meet goals and objectives. Flexibility is a key hallmark of a learning organization as staff analyze work processes, encourage innovation, and try out new ideas. Staff learn to take calculated risks and understand that some experiments will not be successful. Managers understand that taking risks and trying new ideas is an important part of innovation and not trying is worse than trying and not succeeding.

Peter Senge, the expert in this area, "in his book, *The Fifth Discipline,* outlines five component technologies or disciplines that are the foundation for building a learning organization. These five disciplines are: shared vision, personal mastery, mental models, group learning, and systems thinking."[6] A leader who is working on creating a learning organization can use emotional intelligence concepts to enhance the organization's options for success.

According to Senge, "personal mastery is the discipline of continually clarifying and deepening our personal vision, of focusing our energies, of developing patience, and of seeing reality objectively."[7] Personal mastery is much more than rote learning. "In personal mastery, one learns a new skill and learns how applying that skill to the work can move the organization forward."[8] For the emotionally intelligent leader, personal mastery matches well with self-awareness and self-management. As a leader learns more about his or her emotional responses and learns how to manage the responses the more the leader will be able to understand the reality of the organization. That is, when a leader is not hijacked by emotions and thereby responds inappropriately to a situation, the leader is better able to analyze the situation and respond in ways that will be successful.

The discipline of mental models "refers to the assumptions and generalizations that influence how one understands and interprets the organization."[9] In the area of emotional intelligence, it is important for leaders to understand the assumptions they make about interactions with others and to assess the validity of those assumptions. For instance, if a leader anticipates a negative response from a staff member based on a previous encounter, the leader may not listen as carefully as he or she could. The staff member may sense frustration on the part of the leader and wonder why the exchange is not going well, even if the staff member has not made any negative statements. For leaders, understanding their own assumptions about the workplace, about employees, and about the environment are keys to developing a high level of emotional intelligence. Understanding their own mental models can help leaders improve their emotional intelligence.

A shared vision "makes it possible for members of the organization to understand the future they want to create."[10] Leaders who practice good interpersonal skills, and who understand how emotions impact interactions, will be more likely to succeed in working with the organization to create a shared vision. When ideas can be exchanged and interactions among the staff and management are mostly positive, the organization is better able to create and agree to a shared vision for success.

Team learning "is another key component of the learning organization as teams are the fundamental learning unit."[11] Again, successful team interactions are more likely to occur in units where team leaders and team members understand the underlying emotions that can make for positive interactions and good group work. Groups learn to suspend assumptions about how things are done, act as colleagues, and put aside defensiveness to create an open environment for dialogue and discussion when they practice the good social skills of emotional intelligence.[12]

Systems thinking is the fifth element of the theory. Systems thinking "helps bring the concepts of the learning organization together."[13] With systems thinking, "an organization can begin to see that familiar solutions no longer solve problems, that cause and effect are not closely related in time and space, that small changes can lead to big results, and that there is no blame."[14] For the emotionally intelligent leader, systems thinking reminds the leader of the importance of using all of his or her intelligences, skills, and abilities to steer the organization through changes, innovations, and improvements.

By combining the skills and abilities of emotional intelligence with the five disciplines of the learning organization, the leader can create an organization that embraces learning and moves beyond the mechanics of the theory to truly change the organization. Emotional intelligence can be the difference between a good leader in a good learning organization and a great leader in a great learning organization.

LEADERSHIP THEORIES

Beyond organizational theories, one can also review leadership theories to determine how emotional intelligence fits within the various theories of leadership. Leadership theories can be categorized in any number of ways. Some theories look at the individual personality, traits, or skills of the leader. Others focus on the relationship between leaders and followers. Some look at how power is distributed in that relationship. Still others look at group processes. From the many definitions and categories of leadership, a general definition of leadership can be formed. In *Leadership Theory and Practice,* Peter Northouse defines leadership as "a process whereby an individual influences a group of individuals to achieve a common goal."[15]

The key elements of this definition are that leadership is a process rather than a trait and that leadership involves influence to achieve goals. This definition of leadership leads to the question of how emotional intelligence fits within the various leadership theories. Is emotional intelligence an important part of successful leadership? In this section, a variety of leadership theories will be reviewed to determine if there is a relationship between emotional intelligence and effective leadership.

TRAIT THEORIES

Trait theory assumes that leaders have certain characteristics that distinguish them from non-leaders. Research has identified any number of traits that contribute to leadership. Some of the more important ones are "intelligence, self-confidence, determination, integrity, and sociability."[16] An advantage of trait theory is that it is easy to understand. The disadvantage is that there is no definitive list of traits that researchers can identify. Emotional intelligence, as noted in chapter 1, is more than a way of behaving or set of traits. It is the process used to manage one's own emotions and to understand and influence the emotions of others.

MCGREGOR THEORY X AND THEORY Y

In *Human Side of Enterprise,* Douglas McGregor proposes two theories of motivation.[17] In Theory X, supervisors assume employees are not motivated and work only when the work is highly structured, rules are in place, and the supervisor keeps a close eye on the employees. The supervisor is concerned with production rather than with the people in the organization. In this theory, emotional intelligence has little if any impact on the approach of the supervisor. In Theory Y, supervisors assume employees are self-motivated and will do a good job. Theory Y leaders are participatory and are concerned with the feelings of employees as well as being concerned with productivity and positive outcomes. In Theory Y, emotional intelligence gives supervisors ways to work effectively with the different employees in the organization.

BLAKE AND MOUTON'S LEADERSHIP GRID

In their theory of leadership, Blake and Mouton outline five leadership styles distinguished by the leaders concern for task or for people.[18] Leaders who are low on task and low on people concerns tend to create an environment where the minimum is done to stay employed. Leaders who are strong on task skills and low on people skills create authoritarian work places that may be efficient, but have little regard for the employees. Leaders who are strong on people concerns and low on task concerns create organizations that function like country clubs. Employees may be happy, but productivity is low. Leaders who are in the middle with some concern for people and for tasks create organizations that survive but are not outstanding. Leaders high in concern for people and for tasks create team environments where work is accomplished and people feel appreciated. These organizations will achieve excellence. From the view of emotional intelligence, a reasonably high level of emotional intelligence could be found in those leaders who create the country club environment as well as those who create highly functional excellence organizations. In the case of the country club, leaders are attuned to the needs of employees and manage the emotional side of the organization. Unfortunately, productivity is not guaranteed in this environment. While the leaders have many of the characteristics of those high in emotional intelligence, the leaders lack the skills that yield good strategic decisions that result in efficient, successful organizations. In the strong team-oriented environment, emotional intelligence will distinguish those leaders who manage the social relations in the organization and their own emotions from those leaders who are not as skilled at recognizing the impact of emotions on the workplace.

PATH-GOAL THEORY

Path-goal theory looks at how leaders motivate employees in order to accomplish organizational goals.[19] The theory centers on the relationship among leadership style, employee characteristics, and the organizational environment. The theory assumes employees are motivated to accomplish tasks they believe will be successful and will lead to rewards. For leaders, the challenge is to alter their own style to meet the needs of the employees and to encourage self-motivation. Four basic styles are included in the path-goal theory. These four styles are directive, supportive, participative, and achievement-oriented. In directive leadership, the leader tells the employee what to do. Emotional intelligence is not a key factor in this relationship. Employees are given instructions, told what the expectations are for accomplishing the task, and what reward they will get for being successful.

In supportive leadership, leaders treat employees as equals and look out for the well-being of their employees. This style is very much centered on meeting the employees' needs. While some aspects of emotional intelligence will be evident in the leader's style, this style will not draw on all of the nuances of emotional intelligence. Leaders concentrate on understanding others, but may not be as aware of their own emotions and motivations as one would expect in a leader with a high level of emotional intelligence.

Participative leaders consult with employees and seek their input on decisions. Emotional intelligence can be helpful in ensuring that the leader hears the input from employees, recognizes when employees may be reluctant to speak up, and finds ways to ensure that the employees' needs are being met.

In achievement-oriented leadership, the leader challenges employees to work at the highest level possible. Here the tasks are complex, the employees are engaged in the organization, and employees want to excel. The leader who can draw on the many aspects of emotional intelligence will be in a better position to create an environment where employees and the leader can be successful. By understanding both the task environment and the emotional environment, the leader can address the ambiguity and complexity of the tasks and of the relationships in the group to develop opportunities for excellence.

TRANSACTIONAL LEADERSHIP

Transactional leadership, as defined by James MacGregor Burns, describes the leadership relationship as a transaction or exchange of goods and services between the leader and the employees.[20] Leaders provide monetary compensation, benefits, and rewards in exchange for the work performance of the employees. The exchange relationship creates good organizations that can meet goals. It is unlikely to create great organizations as employees are not truly engaged in achieving the goals of the organization. The employees are motivated by what they can get from the organization. It is a very self-centered approach to the organization. For emotionally intelligent leaders, transaction-based relations will improve as the leader learns how to use intangible rewards to promote productivity. By learning how to manage the emotions in a relationship or transaction, the leader can achieve a higher level of success.

TRANSFORMATIONAL LEADERSHIP

In transformational leadership, "the leaders and the followers are united in pursuit of common goals."[21] Goals that motivate performance are the shared goals of the organization rather than the goals of the individual employees of the organization. Shared vision combined with shared goals can lead the members of the organization, both the employees and the leaders, to higher levels of achievement, to higher levels of morality and ethical behavior, and to levels of excellence that are not seen in organizations that rely on transactional behaviors and styles. Transformational leaders are passionate about their work and that passion is spread to others. The leaders encourage creativity, risk taking, and serve as catalysts for change.[22]

Emotional intelligence is a key skill for transformational leaders. Self-awareness is crucial for the transformational leaders. Leaders who understand their emotions, skills, and talents will be able to be authentic and honest with their employees or followers. These leaders will understand the impact they can have on others and how their own emotions can affect an interaction or exchange. Further, leaders who also understand and can relate to others' emotions will be able to tap into people's passions and reactions, to promote excellence. The concern for people in an organization that supports transformation leadership is a positive concern that leads to actions that recognize creativity, excellence, and success in achieving agreed-to goals. The concern for people by transformational leaders is as important as concern for task. By promoting both the welfare of the organization and the welfare of the employees, transformational leaders can create great organizations that achieve great goals. Emotional intelligence combined with excellent technical and political skills gives a leader a wide range of abilities to draw on to make the organization a success.

EMOTIONAL INTELLIGENCE IN ACTION: THE CASE OF ELIZABETH I

In *Elizabeth I, CEO: Strategic Lessons from the Leader Who Built an Empire,* Alan Axelrod describes the leadership style of Elizabeth I.[23] Based on his interpretation of her life, he describes a transformational leader with a high level of emotional intelligence. Elizabeth I transformed England from a third-rate power to a major force in the world and established a rapport with her subjects that showed she understood and cared about them as individuals in her kingdom. Although Axelrod does not analyze Elizabeth I's style in terms of emotional intelligence, he provides enough clues that one can conjecture as to Elizabeth's approach to her role as CEO.

Self-Awareness

Self-awareness is the ability to recognize one's own feelings as those feelings occur. People with high self-awareness "understand what is important (to them), how (they) experience things, what (they) want . . . and how (they) come across to others."[24] Axelrod describes these characteristics in Elizabeth I. He writes that she "saw herself as straightforward, plain-dealing, and bound by an invisible power, higher than hers, never to go back on her word."[25] While Elizabeth I could be devious and scheming, she acted in the best interests of her country. She did not crave power for power's sake, but rather as a tool to use to meet her objectives. She understood the world in which she operated and knew how to act to achieve her vision of a successful England. She understood her own values and views and stayed true to those as she ruled England.

Self-Regulation

Self-regulation is the ability to manage one's own emotions. It is the capacity to soothe oneself, move past anxiety and panic, and bounce back from setbacks. Axelrod provides many examples that show that Elizabeth I was able to manage her own emotions. He reports that when she was arrested and sent to the Tower of London by her half-sister Mary I, Elizabeth did not panic. She remained calm and, according to Axelrod, exploited the symbolism of the situation by not protesting. Instead, she sat on the steps of the tower until she was ready to walk in. She took control of the situation and entered the tower on her own terms, controlling her own emotions, and thereby controlling the situation. Her bravery was noted by the citizenry.[26] This incident is one of the more dramatic examples of a leader controlling emotions to retain a sense of power and leadership even at a point of defeat. Axelrod further reports that Elizabeth I did not hold grudges but let bygones be bygones. Rather than being overwhelmed by the hardships of her early life, she used that time to learn, to develop her own style, and to set the stage for her own work.

Another aspect of self-regulation is knowing when to express strong emotions and how to express those emotions without losing control. Axelrod notes a time in 1597 when Elizabeth I was receiving the ambassador from Poland.[27] While she expected a standard ceremonial greeting, she received, instead, a tirade from the ambassador about the war between England and Spain. Elizabeth responded not by losing her temper, but by carefully articulating her anger, answering his charges and stating clearly that she would not tolerate disrespect. She controlled the situation even though she was angry. Emotional intelligence is not a process of denying strong emotions, but rather, like Elizabeth, knowing when to use those emotions appropriately.

Motivation

In emotional intelligence, motivation is "using your emotional system to catalyze the whole process and keep it going."[28] In self-motivation, one is able to garner the energy needed to accomplish a particular goal or complete a task. With emotional intelligence, motivation includes optimism and hope. With these two emotions, one is able to keep going when things are not going well. Optimism helps one center on the goal and work through the tasks that are needed to reach the goal, firmly believing that the goal will be reached. For Elizabeth I, optimism and hope were part of her approach. No matter how difficult her life became, she looked for positive ways to respond, believing that things would work out well in the end. Even in the Tower of London, she kept her sense of humor and remained calm. She did not give in to threats and would not betray others.

Years later, in addressing her troops on the eve of the invasion of the Spanish armada, Elizabeth I continues to show her optimism and describes her own commitment to battle or self-motivation. She is quoted as saying, "I know I have the body of a weak and feeble woman, but I have the heart and stomach of a King, and of a King of England too."[29] Here she identifies her core self-motivation, that of the ruler of England. She also gives her troops encouragement as they head into battle knowing they have her support and faith in their skills.

Empathy

Empathy is an important aspect of traditional people skills. It is the ability to recognize and feel the emotions of others. It helps one understand others' emotional and social needs by being attuned to subtle signals that indicate how others are feeling. Axelrod describes Elizabeth I as a "people person whose charisma...was extraordinary."[30] He goes on to note that she was often described as a good listener, who maintained eye contact, paid attention to people, and talked with not at people.[31]

Social Skills

Handling relationships is in many ways the art of managing the emotions of others. It includes the "ability to meet others' needs, relate to others over time, and exchange information about feelings, thoughts, and ideas."[32] Good social skills are those that create the business definition of strong interpersonal skills and good communication skills. That Elizabeth I had strong communication skills goes without saying. Her ability to relate to other rulers, to the court, and to the common citizen is well documented. Axelrod gives numerous examples of Elizabeth's skills in this area, from carefully listening to a child giving her greetings, to discussing affairs of state with Parliament. She was very thoughtful in her actions and would take breaks in meetings if she needed to think through an issue. This way she controlled her own emotions and took time to consider the impact decisions would have on others.

This very brief description of Elizabeth I provides a way to look at EI in the actions of a leader who helped change the world as she changed her country. She understood the role of emotions in interactions with others and how to use her own skills to survive in a very tumultuous time. She created a strong country and empire while retaining her power, and the loyalty of her subjects. While her actions are specific to her time, her approach provides solid examples for today's leaders on how strategy, values, and emotional intelligence come together to create excellence and success.

CONCLUSION

Emotional intelligence is one of the abilities of successful leaders. It is a key factor that distinguishes great leaders from good leaders. It is also more evident in theories where leaders are aware of and concerned about the feelings and needs of employees or followers. The theories that include leaders having a focus on people as well as tasks are more relevant to the work on emotional intelligence than theories that concentrate heavily on task accomplishment with little regard for the people in the organization.

"Personal influence, the area of emotional intelligence that addresses both our ability to influence ourselves and our ability to influence others, is the essence of leadership."[33]

NOTES

1. Sharon C. Bolton, *Emotion Management in the Workplace* (New York: Palgrave Macmillan, 2005), 13.

2. Lee Bolman and Terrence Deal, *Reframing Organizations* (San Francisco: Jossey-Bass Publishers, 1991), 15.

3. Ibid.

4. Ibid.

5. Joan Giesecke and Beth McNeil, "Transitioning to the Learning Organization," *Library Trends* 53, no. 1 (Summer 2004): 55.

6. Ibid., 56–57.

7. Peter Senge, *The Fifth Discipline: The Art and Practice of the Learning Organization* (New York: Doubleday, 1990), 7.

8. Giesecke and McNeil, "Transitioning to the Learning Organization," 57.

9. Senge, *The Fifth Discipline,* 8.

10. Ibid., 9.

11. Ibid., 10.

12. Giesecke and McNeil, "Transitioning to the Learning Organization," 58.

13. Senge, *The Fifth Discipline,* 6.

14. Giesecke and McNeil, "Transitioning to the Learning Organization," 58.

15. Peter Northouse, *Leadership, Theory, and Practice* (Thousand Oaks, CA: Sage Publications, 2004), 3.

16. Ibid., 33.

17. Douglas McGregor, *Human Side of Enterprise* (New York: McGraw-Hill, 1960). See also Bolman and Deal, *Reframing Organizations,* 53.

18. Robert R. Blake and Jane S. Mouton, *The Managerial Grid: Key Orientations for Achieving Production through People* (Houston, TX: Gulf, 1964); Robert R. Blake and Jane S. Mouton, *The New Managerial Grid* (Houston, TX: Gulf, 1978); Robert R. Blake and Jane S. Mouton, *The Managerial Grid III* (Houston, TX: Gulf, 1985). See also Bolman and Deal, *Reframing Organizations,* 53.

19. Northouse, *Leadership, Theory, and Practice,* 123.

20. Peter Hernon and Nancy Rossiter, ed., *Making a Difference: Leadership and Academic Libraries* (Westport, CT: Libraries Unlimited, 2007), 53.

21. Ibid., 54.

22. Ibid., 25.

23. Alan Axelrod, *Elizabeth I, CEO: Strategic Lessons from the Leader Who Built an Empire* (New York: Prentice Hall Books, 2000).

24. Hendrie Weisinger, *Emotional Intelligence at Work* (San Francisco: Jossey-Bass Publishers, 1998), 4.

25. Ibid., 235–36.
26. Axelrod, *Elizabeth I, CEO*, 34.
27. Ibid., 183–5.
28. Weisinger, *Emotional Intelligence at Work*, 61.
29. Axelrod, *Elizabeth I, CEO*, 84.
30. Ibid., 86.
31. Ibid., 87.
32. Weisinger, *Emotional Intelligence at Work*, 152.
33. Adele B. Lynn, *The EQ Difference: A Powerful Plan for Putting Emotional Intelligence to Work* (New York: AMACOM, 2005), 213.

7

EMOTIONAL INTELLIGENCE AND DIVERSITY IN ACADEMIC LIBRARIES

Camila A. Alire

"Emotional intelligence...involves the ability to monitor one's own and others' emotions, to discriminate among them, and to use the information to guide one's thinking and actions."[1]

Emotionally intelligent leaders in academic libraries should be strong proponents of diversity in their work environment. That is, based on the various concepts of EI, they cannot disregard their role in developing, supporting, and leading a diverse work environment, one representing all types of diversity (e.g., ethnic, racial, gender, sexual orientation, and religious). This chapter examines some of the more basic EI concepts that can be applied to developing and supporting those diverse work environments in academic libraries. It also includes ways EI academic library leaders can change negative emotional climates relative to diversity through team building.

EI CONCEPTS AND DIVERSITY

Much has been written about EI starting with Peter Salovey and John Mayer, who maintain that, since there is a test to determine academic intelligence (IQ), there should be one to determine emotional intelligence (EQ). They developed such an EQ scale that was norm-tested. It was David Goleman who took the concept of EI and applied it to the work environment.[2] In this chapter, Goleman's EI concepts are applied to developing and maintaining a diverse work environment.

He views two sets of competencies for EI: personal and social. Within those competencies fall four subsets (self-awareness, self-management, social awareness, and relationship management).[3] This chapter will concentrate on three of those subsets (self-awareness, social awareness, and relationship management) and link them to both diversity and EI academic library leaders.

Self-Awareness

According to Goleman, self-awareness is the ability of leaders to understand their own emotions. According to EI theory, academic library leaders cannot be socially aware until they are self-aware. In the case of diversity, are they emotionally on board with their own feelings? EI leaders not only understand and embrace diversity but also promote it. They recognize that every person in the library differs in one sense or another. It is those differences that make academic library environments interesting and challenging. As a result of those differences, negative emotional climates can surface. Neal M. Ashkanasy and Catherine S. Daus said it best: "A negative emotional climate in an organization can stymie organizational and individual growth. That fact necessitates strategies for dealing at the collective level of emotional environments as well as the individual level."[4]

To change the negative climate in academic library workplaces, those libraries need leaders who have strong EI traits and characteristics to manage effectively the strained relationships caused by employees who are unreceptive to fellow employees who are different than they are. They hold different sets of values, beliefs, and cultural norms.

It is important to recognize that the organizational culture of an academic library is determined by the collective set of values, beliefs, and norms. According to Jennifer M. George,

An organization's identity derives from and is a consequence of its culture. Through an organization's culture, organizational members develop a collective identity embodied with meaning. In this regard, an increasingly important leadership activity pertains to the development and expression of organizational culture. Organizational culture is embodied in relatively shared ideologies containing important beliefs, norms, and values....[5]

The whole concept of an unhealthy organizational culture can lead to claims of institutional racism. What happens when new academic library employees come in with a different set of cultural beliefs, values, and norms? How are they treated by long-standing library employees who have grown up within the present library culture? These are employees, many who would maintain that they are not racist. Personally, they probably are not. However, if they abide by the organizational culture that is unreceptive to the differing beliefs, values, and cultures of new employees and if they are unwilling to help change that culture, then organizationally, they are practicing institutional racism. George, who supports the concept of cultures clashing, notes that

cultures are infused with emotions and the allegiance to and identification with cultures stem from people's emotional needs rather than from a more "rational" or instrumental perspective. *Violation of norms and values in a culture results in strong emotional reactions* [italics in the original]...[6]

Part of self-awareness is building and maintaining self-confidence. Do academic library leaders have the self-confidence to take risks in supporting a diverse academic library environment? It is definitely risky to extend beyond their comfort zone as well as the comfort zone of their libraries. To remain neutral about supporting diversity is to be risk averse. To remain neutral about supporting diversity is to be EI challenged.

Social Awareness and Relationship Management

Social awareness and relationship management are complementary as they are the social competencies that Goleman categorizes. He defines relationship management as the ability to induce desirable responses in and with others.[7] Leaders cannot claim to be EI leaders if they do not support diversity in their academic library environments. To support diversity, two forms of action encourage academic libraries to adopt EI techniques and instill them in their staff. The first is through interpersonal sensitivity (empathy); the second is through the use of influence and persuasion. Malcolm Higgs describes influence as the "ability to persuade others" and interpersonal sensitivity as the "awareness of others' feelings and how to interact with them using that awareness."[8]

Interpersonal sensitivity is the key ingredient in developing a positive work environment. In a study of academic library directors where they were asked to identify the top two characteristics of various EI categories, the directors responded under the *empathy* category with "treat people with dignity/respect" as number one and "good interpersonal people skills" (i.e., interpersonal sensitivity and empathy) tied as number two.[9]

One would think that treating people with dignity and respect is automatic in an academic library work environment. It is not. There are some toxic work environments where this basic technique is foreign to many of the library employees.

Interpersonal sensitivity and empathy in the case of EI and diversity can be interpreted to mean that EI academic library leaders exhibit a great deal of sensitivity to those diverse employees working in their academic libraries. These EI leaders demonstrate empathy towards female employees, gay and lesbian library employees, employees of color, and the list goes on. In other words, they treat all their diverse employees with dignity and respect. As previously mentioned, these EI academic library leaders serve as strong role models for all their employees.

Regarding the use of influence as an EI technique, it is interesting to note that in the Native American leadership culture, the art of persuasion (influence) is dominant. Native Americans see leadership as a sphere of influence that must be contextualized (emotional, symbolic, and spiritual) to be understood. They use influence through storytelling (spoken word), tradition, and spirituality to persuade others to do something they had not planned on.[10]

The use of influence as an EI technique for academic library leaders is another action that can be applied to long-standing employees. As Robert Kerr, John Garvin, Norma Heaton, and Emily Boyle point out,

Leadership is a process of social interaction where the leader's ability to influence the behaviour of their followers can strongly influence performance outcomes.... The ability of leaders to influence the emotional climate can strongly influence performance.[11]

If academic library leaders are trusted and respected, they can exert a tremendous amount of influence on their employees. They can expect their employees, as part of their job performance, to support diversity in team environments. They can use their influence along with their strong interpersonal skills to influence the negative emotional climate where some employees are not supportive of fellow employees who are different than they are. Moshe Zeidner, Gerald Matthews, and Richard D. Roberts call it "regulating emotions in others," where communicating with others and influencing them can help with managing conflicts.[12]

When writing about the role of emotions in transformational leadership and the connection between that style of leadership and EI, Wendelin Kupers and Jürgen Weibler state that "idealised influence," a component of transformational leadership (defined as the ability to exert influence by serving as a role model), requires specific emotions for leaders to interact with their followers. Leaders need to be empathetic and to exert influence as agents of change.[13] There is no doubt that EI academic library leaders can play critical roles in promoting and supporting diversity in their work environments and in taking the lead to change the emotional climate of their libraries' organizational cultures from negative to positive relative to diversity.

Ashkanasy and Daus discuss preventive EI techniques to change the emotional attitude of a negative organizational culture. Those techniques are very applicable to changing academic library environments that are not supportive of diversity. EI academic library leaders need to work constantly and persistently to affect change in their environments where diversity is not accepted. As previously mentioned, they start by modeling their behavior in efforts to change the negative organizational culture of their libraries and to set a positive emotional tone. Effective modeling behavior can start to change the library environment. Creating "a positive and friendly emotional climate through modeling" is one of the preventive techniques in keeping emotional intelligence a strong part of teamwork.[14]

George maintains that if leaders can manage emotions (theirs and others) they can manage their organizational cultures. It is through leadership modeling that EI academic library leaders can start changing their organizations' cultures to make them more receptive to academic library employees who are diverse. "It necessitates that leaders are able to instill in followers a collective sense of an organization's important norms and values."[15]

EI leaders who have established and maintained positive and diverse academic library environments must constantly be diligent in preventing negative emotions to resurface by promoting the positive aspects of working in that type of accepting environment. Trust and respect continue to play a large role in maintaining such a healthy emotional climate for diversity.

CHANGING THE ACADEMIC LIBRARY WORK ENVIRONMENT

Up to this point, reference has been made to EI academic library leaders using various EI techniques to make their organizational work environments more receptive to supporting diversity. Succinctly stated, leaders are change focused and lead change in a managed way. Leadership requires the respect and support of employees as everyone works to achieve the shared vision and a set of goals that transform the organization.

Higgs believes there is a direct relationship between EI and leadership, particularly in the context of change leadership. In other words, he supports the concept of leaders needing to be emotionally competent to lead change. In creating the case for change and then implementing structural change, he maintains that EI techniques are critical.[16] Higgs also refers to several elements that are important to this chapter, namely strategic leadership, leading change, and leading cultural building.[17] To take this a step further, one could apply all his work on leadership to diversity.

An emotional climate that is not conducive to accepting diversity needs attention and correction. EI academic library leaders who have inherited negative emotional climates will know that change is needed. This refers to leaders who are new to the organization and its environment. If they are truly EI leaders, they will be socially aware of their new environment. They will pay attention to how diverse employees (no matter the type of their diversity) are treated. They will definitely notice if there is a pattern of nonacceptance or discrimination. Socially aware EI library leaders notice overt discrimination in the workplace and are mindful of subtle discriminatory practices. When they sense such a negative emotional climate, they use EI techniques to begin implementing change.

Equally important is the EI library leaders' recognition that in their new academic library environments there might be a complete lack of type of diversity, especially racial or ethnic diversity. Regardless of the excuses for those situations, EI leaders can start implementing change by considering changes in their libraries' search processes, practices, and procedures (including *unwritten* ones). They can investigate their libraries' values and beliefs that might implicate institutional racism and begin to use their power of influence and persuasion to change those norms.

Change cannot take place overnight. However, EI leaders can begin by using the EI components discussed in this chapter to start leading that change strategically. This can then lead to building academic library organizational cultures that are supportive of diversity. Implicit to making changes in a work environment is effective (and strategic) team building.

When leaders foster a work environment that is full of trust, they have created a place where teams collaborate, create, and compromise as situations arise. Through this trust, EI academic library leaders build and guide teams that are effective. EI leaders rely on trust to provide accepting and supportive environments in which diverse employees feel comfortable working with their colleagues in team environments. Trust also applies to those who accept diversity in their library organizations and to EI leaders with the expectation that they will always provide the necessary leadership and nurturing environment that encourages teams to continue to collaborate.

L. Melita Prati, Ceasar Douglas, Gerald R. Ferris, Anthony P. Ammeter, and M. Ronald Buckley do an excellent job of connecting EI to teamwork and change leadership. They maintain that an "emotionally intelligent leader can accurately assess others' emotions and constructively influence those emotions so that team members will embrace change."[18] As they note, much of the team building is tied to team trust, and leaders must have a high degree of emotional intelligence in order to develop and present themselves as trustworthy members of the team.[19]

If EI academic library leaders inherit work environments that do not embrace diversity, they will need to build teams to help them change those unhealthy environments. They will need to utilize every EI component and characteristic they possess to change their library environments. These leaders need to be aware of their own emotions relative to diversity and to know that they serve as role models for supporting diversity in their organizations and the profession. They need to build teams that acknowledge the need to change their work environments to be more accepting of diversity. Furthermore, academic library leaders need to be acutely aware of the social environment throughout their libraries and to pay particular attention to the emotions of employees who overtly oppose some type of diversity and to help them work through those emotions. As the attitudes of library employees begin to change and become more accepting of diverse co-workers, EI leaders can continue to build strong teams that work together for the good of the organization.

The realities of complex work environments are such that there may still be library employees who refuse to support diversity even when it has been included in their library's core values and guiding principles. They can still be held accountable by building into their job performance expectations that support those values and principles. They can then be evaluated on the extent to which they are successful in meeting their performance goals. The worst-case scenario is that their attitudes and poor performance affect successful team building and teamwork, and require progressive discipline. Clearly in such a situation, managerial leaders would work to prevent low morale from spreading throughout a team or organization as well as ineffective performance on part of the team.

CONCLUSION

EI components and characteristics are critical in helping EI academic library leaders to be successful in establishing and maintaining all types of diversity in their academic libraries. For those who are in the process of making their academic libraries more accepting of diversity, remember:

As you form the various constituencies of your own emotional intelligence, you will likely also increase these powers: intuition, the capacity to trust and be trusted, a sense of integrity and authenticity, an appreciation of constructive discontent, *the ability to find breakthrough solutions in difficult circumstances and make sound decisions* [italics in the original], and leadership effectiveness.[20]

Developing and supporting diversity in academic library environments is hard but necessary work. It is challenging to take the lead when there is a pervasive, negative emotional climate relative to diversity. Once successful in developing a positive climate, it still takes a lot of work to maintain that environment. All library directors and their senior management team should see diversity in the workforce as one of the key issues confronting academic libraries that interact and provide services to diverse communities. At the same time, they should recognize that diversity is important internal to the organization.

"There is a dearth of information on leadership experiences of student leaders of color."[21]

NOTES

1. Peter Salovey and John D. Mayer, "Emotional Intelligence," *Imagination, Cognition, and Personality* 9 (1990): 189.

2. Andrew Langley, "Emotional Intelligence: A New Evaluation for Management Development?" *Career Development International* 5, no. 3 (2000): 178.

3. David Goleman, "An EI-based Theory of Performance," in *The Emotionally Intelligent Workplace. How to Select for, Measure, and Improve Emotional Intelligence*

in Individuals, Groups, and Organizations, ed. Cary Cherniss and David Goleman (San Francisco, CA: Jossey-Bass, 2001), 27–28; and David Goleman, "What Makes a Leader?" *Harvard Business Review* 82 (January 2004): 88.

4. Neal M. Ashkanasy and Catherine S. Daus, "Emotion in the Workplace: The New Challenge for Managers," *Academy of Management Executive* 16, no. 1 (2002): 82.

5. Jennifer M. George, "Emotions and Leadership: The Role of Emotional Intelligence," *Human Relations* 53, no. 8 (2000): 1045.

6. Ibid.

7. David Goleman, "What Makes a Leader?" 28.

8. Malcolm Higgs, "How Can We Make Sense of Leadership in the 21st Century?" *Leadership and Organization Development Journal* 24, no. 5 (2003): 278.

9. Peter Hernon and Nancy Rossiter, "Emotional Intelligence: Which Traits Are Most Prized?" *College & Research Libraries* 67, no. 3 (May 2006): 266.

10. Linda Sue Warner and Keith Grint, "American Indian Ways of Leading and Knowing," *Leadership* 2, no. 2 (May 2006): 231.

11. Robert Kerr and others, "Emotional Intelligence and Leadership Effectiveness," *Leadership & Organization Development Journal* 27, no. 4 (2006): 268.

12. Moshe Zeidner, Gerald Matthews, and Richard D. Roberts, "Emotional Intelligence in the Workplace: A Critical Review," *Applied Psychology: An International Review* 53, no. 3 (2004): 378.

13. Wendelin Kupers and Jürgen Weibler, "How Emotional Is Transformational Leadership Really? Some Suggestions for a Necessary Extension, " *Leadership & Organization Development Journal* 27, no. 5 (2006): 371–374.

14. Ashkanasy and Daus, 82–83.

15. George, 1046.

16. Malcolm Higgs, "Do Leaders Need Emotional Intelligence?: A Study of the Relationship Between Emotional Intelligence and Leadership of Change," *International Journal of Organisational Behavior* 5, no. 6 (2002): 199–200.

17. Malcom Higgs, "How Do We Make Sense of Leadership in the 21st Century?" 281.

18. L. Melita Prati and others, "Emotional Intelligence, Leadership Effectiveness, and Team Outcomes," *International Journal of Organizational Analysis* 11, no. 1 (2003): 28–31.

19. Ibid.

20. Robert K. Cooper, "Applying Emotional Intelligence in the Workplace," *Training & Development* 51, no. 12 (1997): 32.

21. Jan L. Arminio and others, "Leadership Experiences Students of Color," *NASPA Journal* 37, no. 3 (Spring 2000): 506, http://publications.naspa.org/cgi/viewcontent.cgi?article=1112&context=naspajournal (accessed May 22, 2007).

8

RESONANT LEADERSHIP IN ACADEMIC LIBRARIES

Camila A. Alire

"Resonant leaders manage their emotions well and read individuals and groups accurately. They consciously attend to people, focus them on a common cause, build a sense of community, and create a climate that enables people to tap into passion, energy, and a *desire* to move together in a positive direction."[1]

Resonant leadership is one of the newer theories and styles that is starting to receive attention in the leadership literature. Why is it, however, critical to the advancement of academic libraries in times of constant transformation? Fiscal restraints, changing technologies, and endless demands for more resources and services are just some of the challenges that managerial leaders face as they lead change and move their libraries in a positive direction. Resonant library leaders can move their employees forward because they manage their own emotions and pay attention to the emotions of their staff. Employing resonant leadership allows library leaders to be more successful in their organizations and in their personal and professional lives.

This chapter concentrates on the characteristics of resonant leadership, dissonance and its causes, and the process for renewal. It should help readers understand how resonant leadership can help turn unhealthy and dysfunctional libraries around and how it can help to sustain positive academic library environments.

RESONANT LEADERSHIP: AN INTRODUCTION

As discussed in chapters 1 and 2, Richard Boyatzis and Annie McKee, together with Daniel Goleman, wrote the seminal work on emotional intelligence in the workplace. What Boyatzis and McKee found when continuing their research on EI leaders is that many of those leaders fell into a state of dissonance, both personally and organizationally. These authors concentrated on why this dissonance was occurring with EI leaders. Based on what they found through their research and interviews, they developed the theory of resonant leadership.

Resonant leadership is solidly based around the four domains of EI leadership: self-awareness, social awareness, self-management, and relationship management.[2] These domains collapse into two main competency areas:

- *personal competence:* how leaders manage their own emotions (self-awareness and self-management)
- *social competence:* how well they move their employees forward by managing their emotions and by building relationships (social awareness and relationship building)

More specifically, personal competence centers on feeling and thinking, and it helps EI leaders become stronger leaders. Further, it keeps them aligned with their emotions. Social competence is more about relationship building (i.e., team building) and motivating others. Boyatzis and McKee maintain that the leadership competencies that fall under the four EI domains are all relevant to resonant leadership (see appendix A for the leadership competencies).[3]

Although all resonant leaders are EI leaders, not all EI leaders are resonant leaders. This is what Boyatzis and McKee found so very puzzling. How could strong EI leaders who have been successful in implementing, maintaining, and encouraging emotional intelligence in the workplace eventually fall into complete dissonance and burn out? This was important to investigate because leaders who become dissonant were totally out of sync with and alienated from others in their organizations as well as in their personal lives.

According to Boyatzis and McKee, resonant leaders are not afraid to pioneer new pathways for the good of the organization; to do so, they must be inspirational and hopeful. They maintain a balance between giving to their organizations and taking care of themselves in the process.[4] This is what resonant leadership is all about. Being or becoming a resonant leader, dealing with leadership dissonance, and leadership renewal are the themes covered in this chapter.

ON BEING A RESONANT LEADER

As McKee and Boyatzis comment, "leadership is exciting, but it is also stressful. It is the science of power and influence—and power creates a distance between people."[5] That said, leading any organization today includes dealing with constant crises and requires a lot of responsibility. Academic library leadership is no different. Library leaders would be well served by considering resonant leadership as part of their leadership portfolio.

Because resonant leaders are EI leaders, they possess a high level of emotional intelligence, enabling them to keep their emotions in check and to be in tune with the emotions of those around them. They can effectively communicate what needs to be done and why. They do this by building strong relationships with others and keeping them engaged. Resonant leaders know that their emotions are contagious.[6]

Contagious emotions can either be good or bad depending on the leaders' current emotional status. Positive emotions of resonant leaders can be very contagious and affect the workplace. This is best described accordingly:

When we sense that our leader is excited and hopeful, we feel invigorated and motivated. When our leaders exude enthusiasm, realistic optimism, and genuine concern for us, we have more energy for our work and can face challenges more creatively.[7]

Conversely, negative emotions can also be contagious. Negative emotions such as jealousy, cynicism, and hatefulness can cause dissonance in the workplace. People in academic libraries who are looking for any excuse to sabotage, to be destructive, or to deny any accountability within their libraries will jump on this train of negative emotions.

LEADERSHIP DISSONANCE

As Boyatzis and McKee note, "the constant sacrifices and stress inherent in effective leadership can cause us to lose ourselves and sink into dissonance."[8] EI academic library leaders become dissonant when they start losing patience and do not pay attention to the dynamics in their libraries. There is a price to pay when EI leaders start falling into a state of dissonance. The pressure from negative work environments, the sacrifices leaders make during that process, and the dissonance they start experiencing all contribute to *power stress*.[9] Although stress is a part of leadership, power stress occurs when the crises are constant and there is no time for EI leaders to recover. When times are tough, these leaders tend to work harder, thinking that will help cure what ails the organization. All this causes dissonant leadership and unhealthy work environments.

One of the first studies concerning leadership environments and resonant leadership was conducted on hospital leadership. The researchers found that, in hospital restructuring and its impact on nurses and their patient care, there was a correlation between nurses working in strong resonant leadership environments and less negative effects on patient care. Nurses in these resonant leadership environments were more satisfied and more emotionally resilient in the face of major hospital restructuring than their counterparts working in dissonant leadership environments. Two major implications of their study for hospitals were the need to hire more resonant leaders and the need to provide resonant leadership training for EI leaders already employed.[10]

This research could be analogous to academic library environments. An assumption could be made that in academic library environments where there is strong resonant leadership, the library employees are probably more satisfied and, consequently, these positive work environments affect the quality of services they provide to their students, faculty, and staff.

Boyatzis and McKee offer three reasons for leader dissonance:

1. the Sacrifice Syndrome
2. defense routines (coping mechanisms)
3. unhealthy conditions within the organizations[11]

The Sacrifice Syndrome

According to Boyatzis and McKee, the Sacrifice Syndrome (see figure 9.1) "shuts down our ability to see possibilities because the effects of anxiety, fear, nervousness, and the physical damage to our brains are very real."[12] The syndrome renders leaders totally ineffective because they are so busy with *giving* all the time and striving for excellence that they begin ignoring their own personal and professional well-being. Leaders then find themselves in a negative spiral starting with unhappiness and anxiety and leading to meaningless actions, which then causes chronic stress.

Leaders think they are handling stress well psychologically, but in reality, their chronic stress will manifest itself physiologically and then fall beyond their control. Their brains and hormones go into states of "fight or flight" or "state of high alert," which arouses SNS (the sympathetic nervous system), affects their blood pressure, and shuts down the neural circuits in their brains that normally allow them to be open, flexible, and creative. All of these begin to affect their immune system.[13] In the process of negative spiraling and stress, the leaders blame others for all this and begin to employ defense routines.

Defense Routines

There are many defensive signs when leaders become dissonant. The key ones are denial and laying blame. All other defense mechanisms such as cynicism, overreaction, anger, and vindictiveness spring off these two. Boyatzis and McKee refer to the *fundamental attribution error* where leaders see themselves as successful in all the organizational accomplishments and attribute failure to everyone else.[14] These leaders are in complete denial with the reality around them. They are in full stages of dissonance and denial. Almost everyone has witnessed these kinds of negative, dissonant environments, which become dysfunctional for everyone.

Creating Unhealthy Organizations

How do academic library organizations become so dissonant? Are they so focused on achieving that they tolerate dissonance and denial thinking? In other words, do the ends justify the means? Remember that the focus is not on other types of leadership but on EI leadership, where leaders should be self-aware, aware of others, and aware of their organizations.

Library employees who begin to witness the negative spiraling of their leaders are probably too afraid to say something for fear of reprisals. Other employees might not care; they thrive in these kinds of dissonant environments because no one is held accountable anymore. No one has to take responsibility for his or her own actions or actions in their departments.

Boyatzis and McKee refer to the CEO disease where employees will not tell their leaders that there is trouble in paradise. They either view the CEO as invincible or are too afraid to tell them because the CEO is unapproachable.[15] The leaders probably do not realize this and are the last to know. As EI leaders, they have been so busy and focused on *achieving* that they have totally lost sight of what constitutes resonant work environments.

For academic library leaders, this means that those who are spiraling downward into complete dissonance affect their entire library organizations. Staff notice these changes, respond to these negative changes, and model their behaviors around this negative dissonance. The result is the beginning of unhealthy, dysfunctional, and dissonant environments.

When service organizations such as libraries are affected by dissonant leadership, these types of environment affect the people they serve. No one takes pride in his or her work. When things do not get accomplished or when the quality of services diminish, it is somebody else's fault. No one takes responsibility because the library leaders do not. How do library leaders turn their dissonant environment around; how do they return to sound resonant leadership? It is through the process of renewal where change begins (see case study, appendix B)

THE PROCESS OF RENEWAL

As Boyatzis and McKee point out, "To return to resonance and counter the Sacrifice Syndrome, we need to make renewal a way of life."[16] Renewal starts with the process of reviving and sustaining resonant leadership and with the caring for people working in dissonant library environments. Mindfulness, hope, and compassion are the characteristics associated with the renewal of resonant leadership. These characteristics are not mutually exclusive but are interrelated. Although the concentration on mindfulness, hope, and compassion is on renewal, it must be said that resonant leaders use these three qualities to sustain their leadership and manage their strengths. They use these traits to inspire and to help them serve as role models for resonant leadership for their employees.

Mindfulness

Mindfulness as a part of the renewal process is much aligned with EI's self-awareness, social awareness, and awareness of the work environment. Mindful means "inclined to be aware."[17] Academic library leaders need to know who they are and how others perceive them. They must ask what roles they may have had in causing that dissonance. Once they have returned to strong, positive self-awareness, they can concentrate on being mindful of others and their environment.

It is important to mention what being mindful of people and the environment means. How do EI leaders do that, especially those who have been experiencing a period of dissonance? They need to pay attention to what is going on around them particularly by looking and listening. Not only is paying attention to body language essential, but also really listening to what people are saying is important. Being aware of others, however, is not enough; how academic library leaders treat employees is critical. Instilling hope and compassion by their treatment completes the picture for reviving resonant leadership.

Hope

"Hope binds people together and helps us move in concert towards a desired end."[18] Not surprisingly, library employees thrive on the energy of hopeful leaders. They need to know that their leaders see an optimistic future for their libraries. Hope breeds inspiration. Those who refuse to be inspired and do not help move their libraries forward can and should be held accountable.

Boyatzis and McKee see leaders with hope as having dreams and aspirations and as very optimistic because they see the future as realistic.[19] They believe that they can make the changes necessary to advance their organizations. At the same time, they are able to stay in touch with the people around them and lead them forward.

Compassion

Compassion is the third characteristic that dissonant library leaders need to employ to convert their academic libraries from unhealthy organizations to dynamic and future-oriented organizations. Compassion is not just about empathy and caring for others. It is a call to action and once implemented can be very contagious.

Empathy for others is a large part of being compassionate. By connecting with others, library leaders are in tune with their employees and can lead them out of dissonance. There is a reason why compassion can be a renewing agent. It decreases the leaders' stress levels while at the same time increases their effectiveness. Leaders can cultivate compassion by serving as its role model and by making it part of their vision.[20]

It is no wonder that compassion is contagious. Academic library leaders need to view this characteristic not as a soft skill, but as a skill that is essential to turning their libraries around. Mentoring and coaching are prime examples of utilizing compassion to affect library organizations. Because mindfulness, hope, and compassion are characteristics of resonant leadership, establishing resonant relationships is critical in coaching.

Library leaders need to understand that the investment in time to mentor and coach is well worth their time. Reviving dissonant libraries is time consuming and in the beginning might be done person by person. When library leaders coach members of their management team, then positive role modeling begins. Those key managers in turn use the same coaching characteristics (mindfulness, hope, and compassion) to coach their staffs. To reverse Boyatzis and McKee's concept of negative spiraling, this coaching can cause positive spiraling in their library organizations. All of this defines the process for major change from dissonant libraries to resonant ones.

INTENTIONAL CHANGE

According to Boyatzis and McKee, "part of the challenge of creating and sustaining excellent leadership is to recognize, manage, and even direct one's own process of learning and change."[21] Two key questions become, "How do leaders build resonance in academic libraries that are performing poorly?" and "How do they make that change?"

Boyatzis and McKee introduced the intentional change theory/model in which they presented Boyatzis' five major discoveries that were developed from the results of longitudinal studies on sustaining change. These discoveries are cyclical and start with the idea self (what you want to be); the real self (who you are); a learning agenda (identifying your strengths and weaknesses; experimenting with new behaviors (to include EI social awareness); and developing trusting relationships. "Your path to renewal and resonance involves cycling through these discoveries to become the person you want to be and live the life you want to live."[22]

These discoveries make sense and are in line with EI and resonant leadership theory. Academic library leaders need to know and understand themselves before they can understand and work with others and affect change in their library organizations.

CONCLUSION

Critics are quick to view resonant leadership characteristics as soft skills for leading. Quite the contrary, much of resonant leadership (and EI leadership) is common sense, and common sense is not a soft skill. What is so soft about academic library leaders knowing themselves well enough to recognize their strengths and to work on their weaknesses? The leaders also know that they need to treat people the way they would like to be treated. These characteristics make a lot of sense for developing and maintaining resonant library environments

EI academic library leaders now know that they cannot stop with EI leadership; they need to incorporate resonant leadership into their personal and professional lifestyles. Being mindful, hopeful, and compassionate in everything they do will serve them well in leading their academic libraries. It is not too late for those EI academic library leaders who are in a state of dissonance to transform themselves into energized, resonant leaders and to turn around their unhealthy and dysfunctional libraries. They can start by considering the following:

"Any kind of personal transformation that ultimately results in you becoming a more resonant leader—and sustaining that success—begins with some kind of a challenge to your mindfulness and a growing awareness of your passion, beliefs, duties, and your true calling."[23]

NOTES

1. Richard Boyatzis and Annie McKee, *Resonant Leadership: Renewing Yourself and Connecting with Others through Mindfulness, Hope, and Compassion* (Boston: Harvard Business School Press, 2005), 22.

2. Daniel Goleman, "What Makes a Leader?" *Harvard Business Review* 82, no. 1 (January 2004): 88.

3. Boyatzis and McKee, *Resonant Leadership,* 28–30.

4. Ibid., 2.

5. Annie McKee and Richard E. Boyatzis, "Inspiring Others through Resonant Leadership," *Business Strategy Review* 17, no. 2 (2006): 17.

6. Annie McKee and Dick Massimilian, "Resonant Leadership: A New Kind of Leadership for the Digital Age," *Journal of Business Strategy* 27, no. 5 (2006): 45–46.

7. Boyatzis and McKee, *Resonant Leadership,* 24.

8. Ibid., 58.

9. Ibid., 7–8; Annie McKee and Richard E. Boyatzis, "Renewing and Sustaining Leadership," *Leader to Leader* 40 (2006): 30–31.

10. Greta Cummings, Leslie Hayduk, and Carole Estabrooks, "Mitigating the Impact of Hospital Restructuring on Nurses: The Responsibility of Emotionally Intelligent Leadership," *Nursing Research* 54, no. 1 (January/February 2005): 9–11.

11. Boyatzis and McKee, *Resonant Leadership,* 40–50.

12. Ibid., 61.

13. Ibid., 40–44.

14. Ibid., 44–48.

15. Ibid., 65.

16. Ibid., 71.

17. *Merriam-Webster Online Dictionary* (2006–2007), http://mw1.merriam-webster.com/dictionary/mindfulness (accessed May 15, 2007).

18. Boyatzis and McKee, *Resonant Leadership,* 75.

19. Ibid., 152.

20. Ibid., 184–89.

21. Richard E. Boyatzis and Annie McKee, "Intentional Change," *Journal of Organizational Excellence* 25, no. 3 (2006): 49.

22. Ibid.; Boyatzis and McKee, *Resonant Leadership,* 88.

23. Ibid., 204.

APPENDIX A: EMOTIONAL INTELLIGENCE COMPETENCIES AND DOMAINS*

Personal Competencies

1. Self-awareness Domain

- Emotional self-awareness—knowing your emotions and their impact
  - Gut/intuition plays a role
- Accurate self-awareness—knowing your strengths and limits
- Self-confidence—knowing your self-worth and capabilities.

2. Self-management Domain

- Emotional self-control—keeping your emotions under control
- Transparency—honesty, integrity, and trust
- Adaptability—able to change based on the challenges/situations
- Achievement—drive to improve self and strive for excellence
- Initiative—action
- Optimism—half empty or half full.

Social Competencies

3. Social Awareness Domain

- Empathy—paying attention to and dealing with others' emotions
- Organizational awareness—political context and related factors ("decision networks")
- Service—meeting customer needs

4. Relationship Management Domain
- Inspirational leadership—motivating with a compelling vision
- Influence—using different methods of persuasion
- Developing others—helping them grow by giving them feedback
- Change catalyst—designing and leading change
- Building bonds—cultivating/maintaining the various relationships
- Teamwork and collaboration—building teams and cooperation

APPENDIX B: CASE STUDY—C IS FOR CHANGE, D IS FOR DISSONANCE

Laura has been the university librarian of Logan Library, a medium-size university library, for several years. She considers herself an EI leader and had been successful as such in her previous library. Logan Library was in pretty good condition organizationally when Laura arrived; but change was needed, and there was a lot of attention needed in terms of vision, mission, and strategic planning work. Additionally, the university wanted Laura to focus on the library meeting the requirements for membership in a regional consortium. Laura's hands were full.

As an EI leader, Laura had coached her associate university librarians (AULs) to reach their full potential in the three years after her arrival. The success of that coaching allowed them to move into university librarian positions elsewhere within a year of each other. Consequently, Laura had to hire two AULs in her fourth year.

However, in the meantime, even though she had one interim AUL, Laura was overcome with responsibility not only for her duties as the university librarian, but also for the duties of the vacant AUL position. Always driven to succeed, Laura kept adding new responsibilities to her plate while instituting the strategic plan, working on the consortium requirements, and leading the library. Although Laura was an EI leader, she did not have time to focus on social awareness much less on her own self-awareness; consequently, she was out of sync with her employees' emotions as well as her own.

This was all exacerbated by the fact that when Laura was able to hire the second AUL, jealousy and disagreement began to surface between the two new AULs. Both AULs were competing for Laura's attention and approval. Again, Laura was not in tune with her emotional environment to attend to this situation early on.

The AULs' divisiveness continued to escalate to the extent that their departments were not only fighting with each other, but they were also fighting internally. Student employees in the various departments were affected. The quality of services continued to drop such that Logan Library was the talk of the campus. Accountability for services was someone else's problem. No one wanted to use the library itself because of the rude behavior of employees at the various service desks. They were just happy that much of what they needed was available electronically.

The AULs encouraged this dissonance by continuing to fight for status within the library and for Laura's attention. They were good people, but unfortunately, they were not recipients of the same coaching that Laura had provided to her previous AULs. She was too busy being results oriented.

Laura attributed all this discontent to library employees not willing to change and adopt that new strategic plan and mission. She was going to show them; she would work harder to implement the strategic plan and affect change in the library. She was in a total state of denial and ignored the reality of a dissonant library organization and the role she played in it.

Laura was psychologically strong and believed that all this was a passing phase. Her campus friends began to disappear because Laura was not herself anymore.

At the height of dissonance, the provost called her in to talk to her about concerns he was hearing from the university faculty, students, and library staff. Laura was stunned by what she heard. Six months later, Laura began to suffer from asthma. She had not had an unhealthy bone in her body prior to that.

Questions to Consider

1. What could have Laura done early on even before her two AULs began their infighting?

2. How can Laura recover from this state of leadership dissonance?

3. What role could have Laura's campus friends played?

9

ACADEMIC LIBRARY DIRECTORS OF COLOR AND THEIR MEANS OF SELF-RENEWAL

Cheryl Metoyer and Peter Hernon

"Minority leaders bring cultural competencies to their positions."[1]

Emotional intelligence, which is directly linked to leadership effectiveness, involves managing the mood and performance of an organization as well as developing the capabilities of those formally recognized as organizational leaders. It has much in common with transformational leadership, as both theories address planned organizational change and better meet a shared vision.[2] Because leaders who serve as chief executives may find it difficult to sustain their effectiveness over time, given the "unprecedented challenges that can result in a vicious cycle of stress, pressure, sacrifice, and dissonance,"[3] resonant leadership is an important companion theory. As noted in chapter 8, this type of leadership addresses renewal—developing practices related to habits of mind, body, and behavior that enable leaders to develop and sustain resonance in the face of constant challenges.[4] As Annie McKee, Frances Johnston, and Richard Massimilian point out,

When leaders face power stress over the long term and cannot find ways to manage its downside, they risk becoming trapped in the Sacrifice Syndrome, a vicious circle leading to mental and physical distress, and sometimes even executive burnout. . . . [They] may find that things begin to slip at work and/or at home: small problems may seem more than usually troublesome; relationships may become strained; self-confidence may slip and physical health may suffer as well.[5]

PROBLEM STATEMENT

Resonant leadership addresses the need for effective leaders to "engage in a conscious process of renewal both on a daily basis and over time"[6] and how to do so effectively. No study has applied the theory of resonant leadership to academic library directors of color. This chapter reports on a small-scale study of academic library directors who are African American, Hispanic, or Native American and how they engage in self-renewal and restoration (the mindfulness of self and others, the display of hope, and the exercise of compassion). What suggestions do they offer other senior managers within their organizations and other library directors, regardless of their race and ethnicity, about self-renewal? How well do the findings relate to the theory of resonant leadership?

As more culturally diverse librarians prepare for (and assume) leadership positions as library directors and members of senior management teams in libraries, it is important that they (or anyone for that matter) continue to develop leadership knowledge, abilities, and skills and to recognize the importance of ongoing renewal. Awareness, however, must be accompanied by techniques that enable them to cope with (and not be consumed by) "constant crises, heavy responsibilities and perpetual need to influence people.... [After all,] leaders cannot sustain their effectiveness if they cannot sustain themselves."[7] Furthermore, if they are "in the grip of the Sacrifice Syndrome,... the dissonance they create will spread to those around them."[8] Renewal is not a personal weakness, and through it people can calm themselves and resolve inner turmoil without requiring large blocks of time away from work.

Although resonant leadership is a relatively new concept, some research on it has been reported in the literatures of the health sciences, education, and management. Resonant leadership has a positive affect on the heath and well-being of nurses and their patients,[9] and it helps to foster collaborative leadership among elementary school teachers.[10] A recent study demonstrated that, when Native Americans work in their tribal cultures, the prevailing Western models of leadership do not apply adequately. In these cultures, more attention is given to the community than to the individual. Leadership comes more from applying persuasive techniques and from tribal elders and councils.[11] However, while such insights are important, they are less relevant here because this study does not examine tribal colleges or other specialized environments; rather, it looks at culturally diverse leaders of traditional library organizations.

PROCEDURES

There is no known list of all library directors, be they academic or other, who are African American, Hispanic, or Native American. Given this situation, Camila Alire, dean emeritus of the University of New Mexico, and library consultant Elizabeth Martinez were asked to identify a study population of directors who are recognized in the profession as leaders in academic institutions ranging from community colleges to research universities with whom they were familiar. Excluding two directors who had recently announced their retirement, the population consisted of eight individuals. They were contacted and asked to participate and to suggest the names of others whom they consider to be leaders. Two additional names were forthcoming. Of the ten individuals, two declined for personal reasons and one agreed to participate but dropped out. Of the seven participants, five are African American, one is Hispanic, and one is Native American.[12] Viewed from a gender perspective, four are women.

Because it was impossible to observe the directors for a prolonged length of time and to visit each campus, completion of a diary, which is "a kind of self-administered questionnaire...[that] places a great deal of responsibility on the respondent,"[13] became a suitable means of data collection. The directors were asked to keep the diary for a two-week period in September, October, or November of 2006, and to record those activities related to self-renewal (see chapter appendix). The directors reviewed the written summary of their diary entries for accuracy and to ensure their identity was sufficiently disguised. They also participated in a telephone interview, which inquired about other means of self-restoration and renewal that they practice throughout a given year, and examined how they encourage other senior managers and library directors to renew themselves.

DIARY SUMMARIES

Director Diaries

Director One

When not traveling, this university library director begins each workday morning engaged in physical exercise (for 30 minutes), which enables him to start his day "refreshed and energized." He concludes every evening by reading for 30 to 60 minutes ("end my day with something on my mind besides work"). If he travels, he still reads before going to sleep. The other regular activity occurs when both he and his wife are home; "we have family dinner together as a means of communication, relaxation, reflection, and family planning/management."

During every workday he finds time for some other activity. It might be attending:

- a planning or finance meeting of a local charity ("takes me away from work and gives me a sense of giving back to my community")
- a meeting of the Rotary Club ("gives me a sense of civic leadership and giving back to my community through an organization focused on community and world development")

- a diversity seminar ("prepares me to deal (intelligently, effectively) with myriad issues such as diversity in the workplace and beyond")
- a musical performance ("relaxation, reflection, inspiration, and renewal")
- an art museum opening ("cultural and emotional development, in addition to serving as a trustee to this central cultural heritage institution in my community")

He might also have lunch with a friend ("sharing my insights gives me a true sense of the gift of friendship") or attend some school activity for his daughter or drive her to the dentist ("gives me a sense of being a supportive parent").

During data collection, he attended a professional meeting, which gave him "an opportunity to meet colleagues, plan the work of the organization, and leave with a sense of direction and accomplishment." Using e-mail while traveling gives him "a sense of professional responsibility."

On the weekend, he works around the house but finds time to watch sports or a movie, to spend time with his wife and family, or to have dinner with colleagues ("renewal of personal and professional friendships"). He views these activities as relaxing, enjoyable, and taking "pride in my house." He might also relax in a hot tub with his wife, which "provides quality time for reflection, enjoyment, relaxation, and family planning."

Another way to look at renewal is to estimate the amount of time he devotes to it each day. During the workweek (when not traveling), the amount of time ranged from 2 1/2 to 6 1/2 hours, and on the weekend from 3 1/2 to 8 hours.

Director Two

With this director, three activities are most likely to recur on a regular basis: meditation, reading, and walking. Meditation is a "way to relax, [calm herself before attending a meeting,] reduce stress, [and get physical stimulation]," whereas reading provides "nourishment to my body." She walks to and from work every day—"walking is a part of my daily routine." The exercise enables her to start her "morning with a purpose" and to have "a sense of accomplishment." Walking home "helps me to decompress, revisit decisions made, or think through issues. I am very relaxed when I arrive home. I have also gotten in my exercise for the day." Collectively, these activities enable her to "focus on life outside of work."

In the diary she also mentions falling asleep listening to soft music, cooking, and communicating with family members. On weekends, she runs errands; goes food shopping; spends time with her spouse, including taking a walk to "keep in shape," to reflect, and discuss personal activities; attends church, and might watch a movie or have lunch with a friend. "I always spend a couple of hours on Sunday preparing for the workweek. I review my schedule, make a 'things-to-do' list, and do some e-mail."

She refers to one day of the workweek in the diary as "very busy. I missed not doing my mediation and walk to work." As a consequence, she felt "less calm."

The amount of time spent on renewal during the workweek varies from approximately 1 hour to 2 1/2 hours. The amount spent on weekends is considerably more—at least 4 hours.

Director Three

Due to privacy concerns, some activities are not identified. Because she owns horses, she devotes time (both weekdays and weekends) to their care and feeding. On weekends she takes a morning walk with her dogs. This activity provides exercise, connects her to her dogs and the outdoors; "I often pray or talk with the Creator during these walks....I feel centered when I come home....I have gone for walks with dogs my whole life and it truly is a constant in my life." She finds cooking "relaxing (and I like the outcome too)." On Saturday she also takes a nap, watches television, and listens to music. The following day she watches a morning news program while cooking and doing the dishes. She also goes horseback riding, which she finds relaxing and energizing; furthermore, "it connects me with my horses."

During the workweek, she engages in the following activities:

- driving to or from work. She might listen to an audio book. "I have little time to read so [I] use talking books to 'read'. I also remember books better if I hear them. [This] stimulates my mind...and gives me an opportunity to read novels." She might also take a commuter van home and nap during the drive, or she might drive herself to and from work, but without listening to the radio. She appreciates the quiet time and the beauty of her surroundings. "I get to work relaxed, calm, and mentally sharp."
- taking a walk. The walk might take place around a track with a friend, who is an elder. She learns about "the nation, families, language, culture, and history....I am his eyes since he has lost much of his vision and I tell him what is around us as we walk."
- talking with family, friends, or co-workers. Communication strengthens personal and work relationships.
- feeding campus dogs and cats. She does this every day—talking to them, petting those who will let her. "They are so appreciative and look to us for help. I am glad I can help."
- listening to music while she falls asleep at night.

She might also sit on her front porch in the evening ("Sometimes I just need to be still with my own thoughts") or walk around her place ("listening to the sounds of the night").

During the weekdays she spends between 1 and 3 hours engaged in self-renewal. On weekends the amount of time ranges from 2 1/2 to more than 6 hours.

Director Four

This director is actively engaged in physical exercise, in particular, walking or using exercise equipment. He takes a 90-minute walk every evening (with one exception) after dinner. On many mornings, he uses exercise equipment from 6–6:30 A.M. He might also walk home for lunch (a 45-minute walk), and he makes an effort "throughout the day to walk up and down three flights of steps, walk to [campus] meetings..., and maintain a healthy diet." Lunchtime walks help him to relax "from [the] work environment," and all the exercise contributes to "a healthy lifestyle."

Since he has a ranch, on weekends he goes there, unloads and stacks "in [a] shed twenty fifty-pound bags of cattle feed," and loads cattle feed onto a truck. The physical work, he believes, diminishes the likelihood of "mental stress," while using the exercise equipment enables him to be "physically and mentally alert" and to "tone my muscles." For a Saturday football game (home game for the university), he "assisted with the chain markers.... Over three hours...[he walked] back and forth along the sidelines. [This was] physically tiring, but one of the better places to watch the game." Collectively, the assorted activities keep his "mind off my weekday responsibilities."

During the workweek, he spends between 2 1/2 and 3 hours per day engaged in some form of exercise. This does not include the time spent walking in the library and around campus. On weekends, the amount of time ranges between 3 and more than 7 hours. The number seven appeared twice: one for the day of the football game and the day he went to the ranch to cut trees for firewood. This was the day he did not walk in the evening; he was tired from all the "walking, bending, and lifting."

Director Five

This director began recording her activities while attending a library conference on library assessment. As she remarked,

The first day of the conference has been stimulating, rewarding, and physically restful. (My days are usually physically and mentally hectic at work);

One of my rationales for attending conferences of this type is to have [an] opportunity to hear, experience, and participate in the innovative thinking of other...libraries in new ways to manage in a concentrated and stress free environment. I sometimes consider such conferences to be both learning opportunities and relaxation periods and a means of changing the pace from the typical work week and day.

I considered this particular conference to be a means of "getting away" and renewing myself at the same time that I am learning and/or contributing.

On this trip, there were also opportunities to touch base with family and friends. Maintaining family and friendship ties has become increasingly important to me as I have matured during the past several years. At this stage in my life and career, I find family and friendship to be an increasingly important aspect of creating personal stability as a means of reducing the pressures of the work environment; and, additionally, to cope with the odd "coldness" of the human environment . . . [where I live as compared to some other parts of the country].

While at the conference, she took a walk in a garden at the host site. She savored being in a place with "wide open spaces, clean air, and a slower pace of life." She also enjoyed the conference reception: the "wine and good conversation on an informal level with the participants." She worked out on a treadmill at the hotel: "exercise has been an important balancing mechanism for me for most of my life, both physically and emotionally. When I do not exercise, I feel that I have lost control of my life and its well-being schedule; and I feel good right now."

At the conference (but also when she returns to the library), a recurring activity involves watching television, especially the Discovery Channel and reruns of comedies and other programs now in syndication. She finds that "watching TV shows that I truly enjoy for intellectual stimulation or emotional relaxation, or that have good clean humor, is always relaxing." She often works crossword puzzles "before retiring for the evening. This is one of my favorite ways of unwinding at the end of a busy day and to continue to build my vocabulary."

For the flight home, she looked for "leisure reading materials. . . . Science fiction is my favorite; today, I shopped for money management and retirement books." On the flight itself, she read departmental reports to lessen boredom and to be prepared to meet with her assistant university librarians on her first day back to work.

The first day back to work, she closed her office door and instructed her administrative assistants not to forward any telephone calls. The "downtime for concentration and cleaning off my desk" lasted two hours. That evening she went out with a friend for drinks and to listen to music; she found these activities relaxing "both physically and emotionally. I believe that it is necessary to schedule play as well as work; although I am not as successful at the latter as I would like to be."

She visits her mother twice a week and on Sundays goes to church: "I attended church . . . for spiritual renewal, guidance, and fellowship." She might also shop for CDs; "listening to good music used to be one of my favorite pastimes before my life became so hectic as an administrator."

During the week, she might engage in aerobic exercise and weightlifting at a local gym, take a leisurely lunch, read the Bible or attend Bible study ("for spiritual support and to increase my understanding of the Bible and Bible history"), or have an impromptu meeting with the new office administrative assistant. Such a meeting is

a way of having a positive impact in terms of how my schedule is managed and in my working relationship with the office staff. It is very distressing to have invitations and calls for meetings not get on my calendar for some reason. It means in essence not only that I may miss or be late for an important meeting, but that I may be unprepared if notification is not placed on my calendar in a timely manner. . . . My staff has been advised to work towards reducing stress in this area for me and for them.

One Saturday, because she had the flu, she stayed in bed. "It felt good mentally and emotionally to take care of myself over the weekend so that hopefully I will be ready for work on Monday."

She comments, "My favorite line when people ask me what I need most in my job is that I need a 'wife.' I am female and have come to believe that it is much more difficult for females to have effective spousal/family support when they are in leadership positions than it is for most male administrators. The lucky dogs!"

Excluding the days spent at the conference, she spends between 1 1/2 and 3 hours per day engaged in some form of renewal. One day she went to a music festival with a friend and closed her office door to catch up on work (renewal lasted 11 1/2 hours). On weekends, she spends at least 4 1/2 hours per day.

Director Six

The diary begins with this director returning from completing a "hectic travel schedule." The night of his return, he relaxed, reading and watching videos on his iBook. His first day back at work, after a one-week absence, there were a number of meetings to attend, issues to address, and memoranda to write. That evening he relaxed with a drink, watched television, and worked on his dissertation, which provided "mental relaxation."

At least once a week, he has a "secluded lunch" in his office so that he can read newspapers, popular magazines, and professional journals. He will often also play a couple of jazz CDs. "I enjoy staying current with news events and popular culture. These activities are mentally relaxing and emotionally satisfying. They recharge me on long work days." Other recurring activities include leisure reading, working on his dissertation, and watching occasional television programs. He just started taking "a brisk walk around campus" with some library staff members for a mid-morning break. "The walk also provided some team-building and bonding time."

He also attended a professional library board meeting, which was collegial, "emotionally satisfying, [and] mentally challenging with mindless and professional chatter and laughs over dinner." Further, he had a phone conversation with a relative, which "strengthens me emotionally;" he reported that this "helps me to put work issues in their proper perspective."

Excluding the days spent traveling or attending the board meeting, he spends between 1/2 and 5 hours per workday engaged in some form of renewal. The days involving longer hours are ones in which he works on his dissertation. The minimum amount of time spent on renewal during a weekend is 3 hours.

Director Seven

The activities that she lists in the diary relate to the following areas: getting together with her husband, colleagues, or friends at a lunch, coffee break, dinner, or an event (a birthday party, university football game, or concert); going to the beauty salon; reading; cooking; doing exercise; and praying and meditating. The lunch and the drive to and from that lunch with a friend, for example, afforded an opportunity for friendship and companionship. She writes, "it was a pleasure driving back to work seeing all the fall colors and enjoying the hillsides." Further, she felt "happy and relaxed. My thinking was more focused the rest of the afternoon. Getting off campus away from the hustle and bustle is rejuvenating and refreshing." On another day, she had lunch alone and relaxed while listening to a CD.

She looks forward to attending university events. For instance, although it is a required activity, she enjoys the university football game and talking with donors and alumni about the university and the library. She also attended a reception for graduate students returning from trips abroad. When she got home that night, she played a game of Scrabble with her family.

On another day, she wrote, "I had an early appointment at the beauty salon" and talked with people there while listening to the radio and getting her hair shampooed and cut. After a busy day at work, she relaxed by reading a mystery novel. She commented, "I have not had a lot of time to read lately. Of course, I had a glass of wine too."

"Cooking is pleasurable to me, and it is a good way to relax at night after a long day. I enjoy my quiet time in the kitchen. My family knows that the experience is therapeutic so they don't bother me." There are numerous references to getting exercise: walking around the library chatting with staff, walking to and from meetings on campus, walking and jogging in a park, going roller-skating, and doing aerobic exercises ("I really hate it [the aerobics] but it feels so good to do, and it was nice to do it with my daughter"). She made frequent reference to "getting fresh air."

She finds praying relaxing and an opportunity to "enjoy the quiet." For 15 minutes on one workday that had numerous appointments, she closed her office door and prayed. "I was much calmer the rest of the day."

Other than the day of the football game, she generally does various activities on Saturday. She might watch television, take a nap, clean the house, or do some gardening. On one Saturday, she "didn't bring home paperwork nor did I check e-mail." She writes, "It was a good, quiet day. I had no stress at all so it was mostly restful and peaceful. I'd like to do this every weekend but it's not possible." On Sunday she walked with a friend, cooked, and talked on the telpehone with her grandmother.

She spends between approximately 1 1/2 and 3 hours per workday engaged in some form of renewal; some of that activity occurs at night. On weekends the amount of time varies greatly. It might be all day on a Saturday and there might be some university or social function to attend. She does not quantify the amount of time on Sundays, but it seems that at least several hours are devoted to exercise, cooking, and being with her family.

Director Interviews

Aspects of Renewal Not Appearing in the Diaries

The telephone interviews reinforce the activities listed in the diaries, but provide some amplification. Director 2 regards Saturdays as a "personal day," one not involving a trip to the library. She also mentions the importance of eating three meals a day and "taking care of the whole person." This director reiterates her enjoyment of cooking (she cooks and sells food for a veterans' group) and talking with family and friends. Director 4 emphasizes the importance of physical exercise and staying healthy, and Director 5 discusses the value of scheduling "time for personal renewal—[just] as you would any other important activity. Take the time because the organizations we manage...will be there long after we are all gone."[14]

Suggestions for Other Directors and Senior Managers

Renewal and reinvigoration on an ongoing or daily basis are important for people such as library directors who confront power stress and who need to avoid the previously mentioned Sacrifice Syndrome. They mention the importance of senior managers knowing themselves and recognizing (and coping with) any sign of power stress. Director 2 comments, "I am an introspective person and pay attention to the warning signs, such as becoming impatient or distracted. Then I say to myself 'enough already' and stop. I attribute this to my training as a social worker." Director 3 advises other leaders in managerial positions to cover the "basics: eat well, sleep, exercise, and drink lots of water." Her other suggestions are to spend time every day with people who feel renewed and to find a professional passion and pursue it. "Renewal will not occur without a passion in your professional life."

Director 4 emphasizes,

I have a group of words that I repeat. They are harmony, cooperation, sharing, and reverence for life. I repeat these words to the staff and remind them to take time for themselves. I tell them that a healthy mind and body are primary and that they cannot do good work unless they take care of themselves.

Directors 2 and 6 note the "need for a sense of humor," while Director 2 adds the ability to laugh at yourself," and a willingness to take time to "think out" problems. Director 4 does such thinking at night, because then you can be more relaxed and make more rational decisions. You will have less stress, for example, as you decide not to fire a problem employee in whom you have invested time and resources. It is usually more productive and less stressful in the long run, if you make every effort in a relaxed manner to retain the person and address the problem without going to the last resort (firing).

Director 1 simply encourages his senior managers to engage in renewal, and he can see the positive results from it in their performance. While in college, he "sat at the feet Martin Luther King and others who instilled in us the importance of giving back and serving. We were told to find a way of leadership that was not just doing a job." As result, he is a major supporter of leaders engaging in community service and broadening their perspectives.

Finally, Director 6 sees benefits to celebrating the library's "accomplishments before going on to the next task" and trying "to take a moment and breathe" and "to model the behavior I want from my staff."

DISCUSSION

Although the directors never referred specifically to the circle of the Sacrifice Syndrome (see figure 9.1), they were all aware that "maintaining health, both physical and emotional—as well as intellectual top form—is in part dependent on how we manage the inevitable pressures of our roles."[15] The study, however, notes the importance of spiritual health to the well-being of some study subjects. Further, the directors recognize that "dissonance spreads quickly to those around us and eventually permeates our organizations." Self-renewal helps leaders and organizations from getting "stuck in a negative spiral."[16] Coping with stress, as the directors studied point out, may come from everyday habits or occurrences.

Diary entries offer evidence that the directors try to avoid symptoms of the Sacrifice Syndrome through regular activities such as:

- attending functions or games for their children
- avoiding getting home later or leaving home earlier each day
- cooking
- discussing problems and issues with their partners
- engaging in prayer and meditation
- exercising on a regular basis
- falling asleep without any problems
- finding time for the things they find enjoyable
- having a long conversation with a friend or family member

The directors studied set aside time every day to engage in renewal. The diary method documents their focus on mindfulness, at least that portion

Figure 9.1
The Cycle of Sacrifice and Renewal*

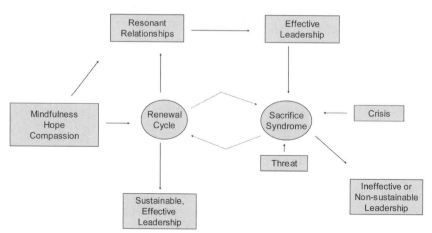

* By McKee, Johnston, Massimilian (Authors), Reprint #9B06TC04, *Ivey Business Journal* 70, no. 5 (May/June 2006): 3. Ivey Management Service prohibits any form of reproduction, storage or transmittal of this material without its written permission. This material is not covered under authorization from any reproduction rights organization. To order copies or request permission to reproduce materials, contact Ivey Publishing, Ivey Management Services, c/o Richard Ivey School of Business, The University of Western Ontario, London, Ontario, Canada, N6A 3K7; phone (519) 661-3208, fax (519) 661-3882, e-mail cases@ivey.uwo.ca. *Source:* Copyright © (2006) by Ivey Management Services. One time permission to reproduce granted by Ivey Management Services on June 20, 2007.

that centers on themselves and not how others perceive them. The method shows the importance of reflection and supportive relationships. There is a direct relationship between mindfulness and physical exercise. The exercise enables them to stay mentally and physically alert as well as to feel relaxed and re-energized.

The diary method does not document hope and compassion, the other two aspects of resonant leadership. The directors express optimism and the awareness of a positive outlook. Their interaction with their partners, families, and friends indicates that they listen. Listening is an initial stage of compassion.[17]

This study shows that renewal is a personal coping mechanism for dealing with the complexity of work and the long hours directors put in, and it might be reflected in many ways. Everyone has different ways of renewing and energizing themselves; recurring themes, however, were the importance of family and friends, physical exercise, and staying focused on life outside of work.

Sylvia A. Hewlett and Carolyn B. Luce distinguish between "run-of-the-mill long-hours jobs and extreme jobs." The latter are positions that are "particularly stressful," and some library directors might meet the requirements of extremity.[18] Hewlett and Luce conclude that "extreme jobs may be deeply alluring, but they are certainly not cost-free....[T]he extreme-work model is wreaking havoc on private lives and taking a toll on health and well-being."[19] Whether or not the directors studied hold extreme jobs, these individuals are aware of power stress and take steps daily to ensure their own renewal and rejuvenation. They have not let the workplace become "the center and source of [their] social lives."[20]

Topics for Further Research

Although the study does not focus on the stressful aspects of work and the pressures that directors face on a regular basis, there is a need for such research and for more examination of any linkage between the circle of the Sacrifice Syndrome and ineffective leaders, ones who do not add value[21] and who detract from the accomplishment of the organization's mission and goals. Perhaps such leaders do not engage in self-renewal, and the consequences of that neglect merits documentation.

The conversations with these directors raise questions for further exploration such as, "Have library directors of color developed skills of resonant leadership and self-renewal as a survival technique?" and "Are library directors from other cultures more likely than directors of color to crease dissonant environments?"

This study, more so than other writings on resonant leadership, indicates that mindfulness, one of the key elements of renewal, may result from normal daily activities or routines. Other studies need to examine other elements comprising resonant leadership, in particular hope and compassion depicted in figure 9.1. Such research might investigate if satisfaction in the accomplishment of one's work furthers renewal, and that research might go beyond a study of directors to examine leadership at different levels of the organization. Are there differences in how leaders at those levels think about and engage in self-renewal? Are some renewal strategies more effective than others? Further, there is a need for in-depth case studies that examine figure 9.1 in its entirety.

Further research might compare culturally diverse managerial leaders in traditional organizations with those functioning in tribal and other special contexts, as well as with directors who are not culturally diverse. Resonant leadership, however, underscores the importance of emotions and how managerial leaders deftly manage their emotions.

The importance of religiosity and spirituality on renewal is not well understood and merits further consideration, especially when they are linked to managerial leadership, a term that applies to managers who are leaders in the broader community.[22] The relationship between renewal and spirituality has long been evident in the practice of religious retreats. Employees might withdraw or retire from the routine workplace to an off-site location. Usually, this alternative location encourages informality, introspection, and creativity through a balanced program of silence, nature, shared meals, some physical activity, and re-ordering of time commitments and schedules.

Another topic for investigation is spiritual leadership theory, which is "in part...a response to the call for a more holistic leadership that helps to integrate the four fundamental areas that define the essence of human existence in the workplace—the body (physical), mind (logical/rational thought), heart (emotions; feelings), and spirit."[23] There are connections among resonant leadership, emotional intelligence, and spiritual leadership, such as the fact that leaders must know themselves. Two aspects of spiritual leadership are spiritual survival, which adds "meaning in life and a sense of interconnectedness with other beings,"[24] and workplace spirituality, which includes maintaining "a spiritual practice (e.g., spending time in nature, prayer, mediation, reading inspirational literature, yoga, shamanistic practices, [or] writing in a journal),"[25] and some unique attributes (e.g., ones related to love).[26] However, each theory attempts "to foster higher levels of organizational commitment and productivity."[27]

CONCLUSION

Leadership focuses on social influence—influencing others to attain group, organizational, and societal goals. The purpose is to motivate people to develop, access, and carry out a shared vision; more than likely one centered on managing change (creating an agile organization that best serves the mission and goals of the parent institution or organization). As managerial leaders address myriad, complex issues, it is critical that effective leadership remains sustainable. As a consequence, it is important for leaders to engage in those resonant relationships they find successful to their renewal. Aspiring managerial leaders, regardless of race, must be familiar with the different leadership theories but they should not discount the value of resonant leadership. With so few African American, Hispanic, or Native American academic library directors recognized within the profession as leaders, it may be that their means of renewal will serve as a model for other library leaders and encourage other people of color to become library directors.

"Visionary leaders need to be adaptable, versatile, flexible, and tolerant of ambiguity."[28]

NOTES

1. Camila A. Alire, "Diversity and Leadership: The Color of Leadership," *Journal of Library Administration* 32, no. 3/4 (2001): 100–01.

2. Peter Hernon and Nancy Rossiter, "Emotional Intelligence: Which Traits Are Most Prized?" *College & Research Libraries* 67, no. 3 (May 2006): 272–73.

3. Richard Boyatzis and Annie McKee, *Resonant Leadership: Renewing Yourself and Connecting with Others through Mindfulness, Hope, and Compassion* (Boston: Harvard Business School Press, 2005), 9.

4. Ibid., 5.

5. Annie McKee, Frances Johnston, and Richard Massimilian, "Mindfulness, Hope, and Compassion: A Leader's Road Map to Renewal," *Ivey Business Journal* 70, no. 5 (May/June 2006): 1.

6. Boyatzis and McKee, *Resonant Leadership,* 9.

7. McKee, Johnston, and Massimilian, "Mindfulness, Hope, and Compassion," 1.

8. Ibid.

9. Greta G. Cummings, *An Examination of the Effects of Hospital Restructuring on Nurses: How Emotionally Intelligent Leadership Styles Mitigate These Effects* (Doctoral diss., University of Alberta (Canada), 2003).

10. Kristi Yorke, *A Study of Leadership Theory in Practice: Implementing a Social Responsibility Program at McGill Elementary School* (Doctoral diss., Royal Roads University (Canada), 2005).

11. See Linda S. Warner and Keith Grint, "American Indian Ways of Leading and Knowing," *Leadership* 2, no. 2 (2006): 225–44.

12. The Human Subjects Division, University of Washington, approved the project in spring 2006.

13. Colin Robson, *Real World Research: A Resource for Social Scientists and Practitioner-Researchers* (Oxford, UK: Blackwell, 1993), 254. For more about the use of a diary as a means of data collection, see Peter Hernon, Ronald R. Powell, and Arthur P. Young, "Academic Library Directors: What Do They Do?" *College & Research Libraries* 65, no. 6 (Nov. 2004): 539–40.

14. Only Director 6 mentioned an annual holiday and how it was a calming and relaxing time.

15. Boyatzis and McKee, *Resonant Leadership,* 51.

16. Ibid., 6, 51.

17. Ibid., 187.

18. Sylvia Ann Hewlett and Carolyn Buck Luce, "Extreme Jobs: The Dangerous Allure of the 70-hour Workweek," *Harvard Business Review* 84, no. 12 (December 2006): 51. The holders of extreme jobs work at least 60 hours per week, are high wage earners, and demonstrate at least five of the following characteristics: "unpredictable flow of work, fast-paced work under tight deadlines, inordinate scope of responsibility that amounts to more than one job, work-related events outside regular work hours, availability to clients 24/7, responsibility for profit and loss, responsibility for mentoring and recruiting, large amount of travel, large number of direct reports, and physical presence at workplace at least ten hours a day" (p. 51). Although it is doubtful that library directors are the high wage earners the authors consider, many of them meet a number of the characteristics.

19. Ibid., 54.

20. Ibid.

21. Boyatzis and McKee, *Resonant Leadership,* 53.

22. For a discussion of the term *managerial leadership,* including its historical development, see Peter Hernon and Nancy Rossiter, *Making a Difference: Leadership and Academic Libraries* (Westport, CT: Libraries Unlimited, 2006), 254–56.

23. Louis W. Fry, "Toward a Theory of Spiritual Leadership," *The Leadership Quarterly* 14, no. 6 (2003): 722.

24. Ibid., 705.

25. Ibid., 704–05.

26. See Ibid., 719 for an identification of the attributes.

27. Ibid., 693.

28. Alire, "Diversity and Leadership," 105.

APPENDIX: DIARY

In *Resonant Leadership* (Harvard Business School Press, 2005), Richard Boyatzis and Annie McKee link resonant leadership to emotional intelligence by stressing the importance of leaders being able "to sustain their effectiveness—and resonance—over time." The key to resonance is one's ability to renew or develop practices (habits of mind, body, and behavior) that enable a person "to create and sustain resonance in the face of unending challenges year in and year out."

We realize that it is impossible to separate your role as library director and leader and therefore we would like you to focus on what you do for renewal as you relieve yourself of work-related stress. We ask you to complete this diary for a two-week period (any two weeks of the months of September–November, 2006). Please complete one form per day and provide sufficient detail about the activity. Data collection begins on a Monday and ends on a Sunday; please indicate what you do during the work day and evening as well as weekend to renew yourself physically, mentally, and emotionally. (You may write on the back of this page, if necessary.) If an activity is private, you may decline from including it. All of the information will be confidential. The Diary will be shredded upon completion of the study.

Date   Activity   Time started   Time stopped

Please state/describe the purpose of each activity.

What impact does an activity have on you physically, mentally, or emotionally?

Any comments

Thank you

10

CONCLUDING THOUGHTS

Peter Hernon, Camila A. Alire,
and Joan Giesecke

"Over the next decade, colleges and universities will have to make critically important practical and policy decisions about the function of libraries, about the space devoted to libraries, and about the role of librarians."[1]

Academic libraries and their institutions are undergoing profound change as noted by many authors and stories in the popular, scholarly, and research literatures. There is increased pressure from different stakeholders for both the libraries and their institutions to demonstrate their accountability, effectiveness, and efficiency with quantitative and qualitative techniques (e.g., the application of performance and outcomes metrics reflective of the perspectives of customers and different stakeholders). Regional and program-accrediting organizations, for instance, might speak of student-learning outcomes and the impact of higher education on what students actually learn. As a result, assessment might refer "to the collaborative process of gathering, analyzing, interpreting, and using interpretations of various kinds of evidence to answer internally raised questions about the quality and effectiveness of . . . programs [of academic] study."[2]

Libraries face increasing competition in the provision of digital resources and services and they are losing their supremacy in the provision of both knowledge and information to their constituencies. Further, the information-seeking behavior of faculty and students continues to change, as do the methods of delivering information to them. Many libraries are forging new partnerships on campus (e.g., a learning commons housed in a library but providing a wide range of campus support services) and with other libraries, and there is more discussion of space planning and the identity of the library in terms of social space, collaborative space, and learning space.

It is sometimes forgotten, as Jerry D. Campbell points out, that, despite such change, the "fundamental purpose" of academic libraries "has remained the same: to provide access to trustworthy, authoritative knowledge" and information as well as to create quality learning spaces and an increased instructional role through information literacy.[3] Complicating matters, digital resources are costly to provide, the library building might be perceived as a "cultural icon," and librarians might be narrowly viewed as guardians of knowledge. Campbell sees a challenge for librarians in transferring their activities and functions to "a new mission designed for a more digital world."[4]

ISSUES CONFRONTING ACADEMIC LIBRARIES IN THE FUTURE

There are a number of excellent overviews of the issues confronting librarianship, in particular academic librarianship, in the new century. One of them focuses on higher education and another on leadership.[5] Much has been written about possible futures and the environment in which libraries will function.[6] One of the more recent views comes from The Council of Higher Education Management Associates (CHEMA). In an opening page, the council's report noted that "heightened competition, changing revenue streams, demographics, technology, and altered public perceptions are creating serious threats and opportunities for higher education,"[7] and, by extension, for academic libraries.

The report notes disagreement over the extent to which the leaders of today are change agents who understand how their individual functional areas will change in the future. The challenges for higher education leaders, as the report discusses, are numerous as they "embrace a broad set of tactics and strategies to prepare their institutions or individual functions for the changes of the future."[8]

In 2001 and 2002, the Focus on the Future Task Force within the Association of College and Research Libraries identified seven critical issues:

1. recruitment, education, and retention of librarians
2. role of library in academic enterprise
3. impact of information technology on library services
4. creation, control, and preservation of digital resources
5. chaos in scholarly communication
6. support of new users
7. higher education funding[9]

Although this list is not comprehensive and the coverage in that article does not reflect the present day very well, the topics are still relevant. For instance, under the first issue, as academic libraries create institutional repositories and become more active in assisting faculty in creating resources for placement in courseware management systems such as Blackboard, more professional staff are entering academic libraries who do not hold a master's degree in library and information science. Further, as libraries engage in succession management, they do not always replace retiring and departing staff with individuals who have similar skill sets and abilities. A number of library directors are hiring professional staff who are receptive to change and who can engage in analytical thinking and problem solving as well as display effective oral and written communication skills.

Two important questions become:

1. How do we attract talented people to the profession who are customer focused, who can meet changing work roles and responsibilities, and who are comfortable (and able to deal) with a library's stakeholders and changing roles?
2. How do we retain such individuals and nurture their development and advancement?

CHANGING LIBRARY ROLES, VALUES, AND VISION

In a presentation for the Simmons College program in managerial leadership in the information professions, James G. Neal, dean of Columbia University Libraries and a professor of practice in that doctoral program, identified the changing library roles as focusing on being a consumer, an intermediary and aggregator, publisher, educator, research and development organization, entrepreneur, and policy advocate.[10] He discusses some of these roles in "The Entrepreneurial Imperative: Advancing from Incremental to Radical Change in the Academic Library," where he proposes that libraries re-position themselves as entrepreneurial organizations and that academic libraries successfully compete in the information marketplace for new business and for corporate, foundation, and federal assistance.[11] "Academic libraries will become," he suggests, "centers for research and development in the application of technology to information creation and use. They will become aggregators and publishers, and not just consumers of scholarly information."[12] Further, these libraries need to create new income streams that enhance the activities, programs, and services that they offer. Doing all of this requires libraries to move "from incremental to radical change."[13]

In his address, he noted that shifting values accompany those changing roles. Examples of those values include assessment; a business plan, which links an agile process to resources; competition; marketing; resource development; self-service, where customers want to do more without any assistance; and strategic action, where the library aligns itself with the parent institution and builds the necessary capacity for the sustainability of its programs and services. Marketing focuses on issues such as the penetration of new markets, some of which hold different values; the diversification of markets; and continuing to serve existing markets well. Resource development, which differs from resource allocation, involves resource attraction and includes leadership in areas such as building and sustaining partnerships. Resource attraction focuses on fundraising, the receipt of research grants, technology transfer, the leasing of space, the sale of products and services, and more.

Clearly, the vision of a library has moved from a warehouse or collection of books and other materials to being a vital partner within the institution, one that cooperates with academic support services and faculty and students. As libraries continue to change, they retain a legacy role while shifting their infrastructure to address the different roles that Neal articulated.

CHANGE MANAGEMENT

Change management focuses on the infrastructure of libraries (staff, facilities, collections, and technology) and the relationship between libraries and the broader environment in which they function. Libraries approach change management from the perspective of their mission, vision, and goals as well as those of the parent institution. The purpose is to enable the organizations to implement strategies that better position them to meet more effectively and efficiently those missions, visions, and goals.

As figure 10.1 illustrates, change management focuses on library roles, services, operations, and staff. Most importantly, it often deals with organizational culture—its norms, values, behavior patterns, rituals, and traditions. As well, there are different perspectives on change management, which include those of the library, its customers, the institution, and stakeholders. Adding to the complexity of the figure is the environment in which libraries function. Environment includes factors related to geography (from local to global), economics, politics, and culture. Further, the arrow in the figure pointing to resources and budget goes in both directions because both affect services, perspectives, and so on. In fact, staff is a resource and the time availability of staff is a resource issue. Criteria of assessment become accountability, effectiveness, and efficiency, and they deal with the environment and library roles, services, and so forth. All of these issues and factors have an impact on innovation and illustrate the need for managerial leaders who combine the skills and abilities to manage an effective organization while moving that organization to accomplish a shared vision, such as the one offered by Rush Miller in his discussion of his accomplishments at the University of Pittsburgh library system.[14]

Figure 10.1
Change Management

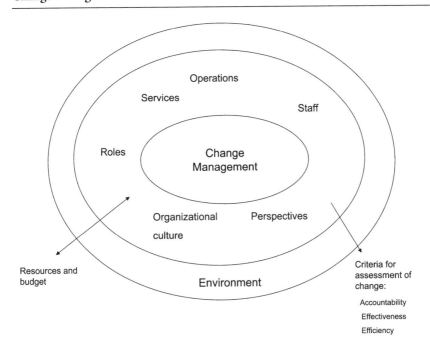

LEADERS IN THE PROFESSION

Within the profession of library and information science, there is a lack of agreement (and perhaps thought) about who are its present leaders. One view, a narrow one, states that the library director, by virtue of that position, is the de facto leader. In fact, that person might be an effective or ineffective manager but not a leader who gets staff and others outside the library to work collaboratively toward the accomplishment of a shared vision. Some staff might predate the hiring of that director or disapprove of what the director is trying to accomplish, and some staff might resist change since they did not participate in the selection of that person as their leader and because they prefer the status quo. Clearly, the concept of leadership is not well understood throughout the profession and in all libraries. Effective directors who are truly managerial leaders support and nurture the development of leaders at all levels of the organization. After all, staff can be both leaders and followers.

Perusal of *Leaders in American Academic Librarianship, 1925–1975* indicates that during those 50 years a number of leaders were active within their institutions and beyond.[15] A complementary list of 100 major leaders in the profession appeared in *American Libraries*.[16] In writing this book and discussing leadership with different individuals in the profession, from beginning librarians to library directors, questions arise about who are the leaders of today and how they are perceived within their own organizations. More importantly, who are the leaders of tomorrow and how well can they interact with different stakeholders as libraries become even more engaged in competition.

BALDRIGE NATIONAL QUALITY AWARD

The Malcolm Baldrige National Quality Award, which the National Institute of Standards and Technology of the U.S. Department of Commerce manages, seeks to build partnerships in the private and public sectors and to improve national competitiveness. The first core concept that applicants must address is visionary leadership, which involves setting directions, creating "a student-focused, learning-oriented climate," presenting "clear and visible values," and having "high expectations." Further,

Your leaders should ensure the creation of strategies, systems, and methods for achieving performance excellence, stimulating innovation, building knowledge and capabilities, and ensuring organizational sustainability. The values and strategies should help guide all of your organization's activities and decisions. Senior leaders should inspire, motivate, and encourage your entire workforce to contribute, to develop and learn, to be innovative, and to be creative.

The criteria call for leaders to be results oriented, accountable, mentors, and role models. "As role models, they can reinforce ethics, values, and expectations while building leadership, commitment, and initiative throughout your organization." Leaders advance "learning-centered education" by building alliances throughout the institution and in the community.[17]

The biggest change in the criteria relating to leadership for its 2007 application is that they contain a quantitative component that addresses performance and what senior leaders accomplish. Clearly, applicants must demonstrate sustainability in the effectiveness of their leadership, as shown in table 10.1. The criteria also identify succession planning as an ongoing responsibility for leaders.

LEADERSHIP METRICS

Reflecting on the criteria for the Baldrige Quality Award and its inclusion of questions requiring the presentation of quantitative evidence, a logical next step is to develop metrics that can be converted to a ratio and percentage. In other words, why not offer a metric (e.g., the number of reference

Table 10.1
Senior Leadership*

Describe how senior leaders guide and sustain your organization. Describe how senior leaders communicate with your workforce and encourage high performance. Within your response, include answers to the following questions:

Vision and Values

- How do senior leaders set organizational vision and values? How do senior leaders deploy your organization's vision and values through your leadership system, to the workforce, to key suppliers and partners, and to students and stakeholders, as appropriate? How do senior leaders' personal actions reflect a commitment to the organization's values?

- How do senior leaders personally promote an organizational environment that fosters, requires, and results in legal and ethical behavior?

- How do senior leaders create a sustainable organization? How do senior leaders create an environment for organizational performance improvement, the accomplishment of your mission and strategic objectives, innovation, competitive or role model performance leadership, and organizational agility? How do they create an environment for organizational and workforce learning? How do they personally participate in succession planning and the development of future organizational leaders?

Communication and Organizational Performance

- How do senior leaders communicate with and engage the entire workforce? How do senior leaders encourage frank, two-way communication throughout the organization? How do senior leaders communicate key decisions? How do senior leaders take an active role in reward and recognition programs to reinforce high performance and a focus on the organization, as well as on students and stakeholders?

- How do senior leaders create a focus on action to accomplish the organization's objectives, improve performance, and attain its vision? What performance measures do senior leaders regularly review to inform them on needed actions? How do senior leaders include a focus on creating and balancing value for students and other stakeholders in their organizational performance expectations?

*National Institute of Standards and Technology, Education Criteria for Performance Excellence (Gaithersburg, MD: National Institute of Standards and Technology, 2006), 16. Available at http://baldrige.nist.gov/Education Criteria.htm (accessed January 13, 2007).

questions answered in relation to the number asked), but this time aim the numerator and dominator at leadership? For instance,

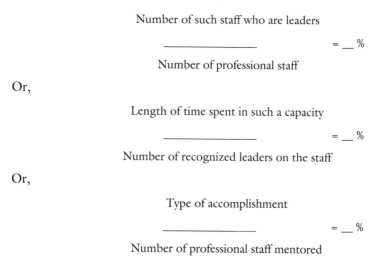

Number of such staff who are leaders

—————————————   = __ %

Number of professional staff

Or,

Length of time spent in such a capacity

—————————————   = __ %

Number of recognized leaders on the staff

Or,

Type of accomplishment

—————————————   = __ %

Number of professional staff mentored

Upon scrutiny, these examples do not sufficiently address leadership as something important, and they are not that revealing. The questions raised in table 10.1 do not adequately address the role and success of senior leaders in contributing to organizational effectiveness. The influence of leaders on making an organization do what it is supported to do comprises indirect activities, ones not easily converted into simple metrics. Organizational effectiveness examines results and not the achievements of leadership in achieving those results. Would libraries comprise effective organization without effective leadership? Leaders promote organizational effectiveness more than they do their role and presence in producing it. At best, leaders leave their footprints on organizational effectiveness, but they should not want organizational effectiveness to be seen as revolving around them. They do not want to create and decree their vision, a shared vision that challenges the organization to improve, like Moses delivering the Ten Commandments. That vision translates into a plan to accomplish that mission; staff must buy into that plan and be empowered to achieve it.

The balanced scorecard, which links organizational performance to four perspectives (financial, customer, innovation and learning, and internal business processes), deals with a measurement system as opposed to a system to manage change and covers organizational effectiveness. The concept does not focus on leadership; it centers on an organization's mission and customers. Any output or results lead to better service for an organization's customers. Leadership is not an outcome.

A better way to isolate leadership and both the capability and effectiveness of individual leaders is through personnel evaluation. Such evaluation might occur annually or at regularly scheduled intervals (e.g., every five years) and might perhaps come through 360-degree assessment that includes the assessment of different stakeholders[18] or one of the instruments identified in chapter 2.

STRENGTHENING ORGANIZATIONAL LEADERSHIP THROUGH DIVERSITY

What would be one of the most helpful components for current or future EI academic library leaders to know about organizational leadership? And yet, what might be the most forgotten component of organizational leadership? One could say it is the diversity component, especially racial/ethnic/ cultural diversity.

Emotionally intelligent academic library leaders pride themselves on recognizing the importance emotions play in the development of others. The two EI domains—social awareness and relationship management (see table 4.1)—deal with how well academic library leaders recognize and manage others' emotions, build relationships, and work in their environments' social situations. It is these two domains that can be tied directly to diversity and organizational leadership.

Organizational leadership can be strengthened if diversity becomes an integral component of academic libraries. That is, diversity becomes second nature in every aspect of academic library work. This is no easy feat.

EI academic library leaders must not only be aware of their own emotions towards diversity but must also be aware of their libraries' emotional climate relative to diversity. They have to lead the efforts to make their library environments accepting of all diverse individuals. Doing this can only strengthen the organizational leadership of academic libraries because academic library leaders have not only embraced diversity in their organizations but they also serve as a role models for supporting and integrating diversity.

Because resonant leadership is a component of EI, academic library leaders become dissonant when they develop defensive routines or coping mechanisms. The two that are pertinent to organizational leadership are self-denial and lack of reality.[19] These two coping mechanisms are more prevalent when dealing with diversity in academic libraries.

Gary Howard identifies four emotions that are counter-productive in any discussion about the realities of diversity in the workplace. Those emotions include denial (diversity as ethnic cheerleading), hostility (organized hate groups), deep fear of diversity (fearing the unknown), and guilt (oppression of forefathers).[20] EI academic library leaders need to deal with those realities in order to strengthen their organizations through diversity. They need to realize that some of those emotions exist in their academic libraries today. They must lead by example and diversity must be a part of their vision.

Academic library leaders can strengthen their organizations relative to diversity by employing the whole concept of EI relationship management.

They could serve as change catalysts by using their influence to develop others into being more accepting of diverse co-workers. Their inspirational leadership could include building bonds between employees and in doing so start building strong, supportive teams.

LINKING EMOTIONAL INTELLIGENCE TO ORGANIZATIONAL CULTURE AND CHANGE

Successful change management aimed at changing library roles, values, and vision involves creating an organizational culture that supports and rewards change. The culture of the organization is one of the most critical factors in determining an organization's capacity to change and maintain effectiveness. "When culture is out of alignment with mission, core values, and operational strategy, it can become a significant liability for the organization."[21] Too often, in creating change strategies, leaders may develop strategies that do not build on the strategies that create emotionally intelligent organizations. They risk alienating employees who feel disengaged from the organization. When employees disengage from the organization, they no longer perform at levels that can lead the organization to excellence.

In the midst of developing change strategies, successful leaders will think through the impact of change on an emotional as well as a rational level. One way to begin the process of considering the impact of emotions is to review the work of Marcus Buckingham and Curt Coffman in *First, Break All the Rules*.[22] In their book, the two authors from Gallup Corporation discuss how to create an organization where employees are fully engaged in working for the success of the organization. They describe 12 factors that impact how employees view their work units. In a system similar to the hierarchy of needs described by Abraham Maslow, Buckingham and Coffman state that first staff need to know what is expected from them and that they have the resources to do their work.[23] These two needs equate to Maslow's safety and security needs. Once these needs are met, Buckingham and Coffman describe the people's need to contribute as individuals to the organization. These needs are similar to Maslow's needs of self-esteem. Once staff feel they can contribute as individuals, staff look to see if they belong and if their colleagues are working hard to succeed. These issues fall into Maslow's social needs. Finally, staff want to know how they can grow on the job. Here the staff are seeking self-actualization as described by Maslow. Throughout this hierarchy of needs, staff react emotionally to their environment. The need to be appreciated as individuals and as members of a group is fulfilled when the relationships within the group are positive. Managing relationships and staff emotions are all part of emotional intelligence.

Buckingham and Coffman describe the Gallup research that shows that when an employee's 12 needs as described above are met, the unit will have a culture that supports and ensures excellence. Employees will contribute to the best of their abilities and the unit will seek to meet the unit's goals and objectives. Employees will be engaged in the organization, a characteristic that includes the intellectual, cognitive, and emotional efforts of each person.

For the emotionally intelligent leader, the challenge is to create an environment that Buckingham and Coffman describe as most likely to yield success. Leaders must find ways to move people's emotions in a positive direction that clears away toxic emotions that can cloud an organization. When leaders are successful in creating positive emotions, they develop an organization with resonance. Resonant leaders hit the right approach that reinforces positivism. "Dissonant leadership produces groups that feel emotionally discordant, in which people have a sense of being continually off-key."[24]

In *Primal Leadership*, Daniel Goleman and his fellow authors outline three key concepts that leaders must consider in creating effective, emotionally intelligent cultures. These factors are: discovering the emotional reality, visualizing the ideal, and sustaining emotional intelligence.[25] Leaders discover the emotional reality of an organization by respecting group values and integrity and linking the change in vision to the center core values of the organization. By keeping the organization connected to core positive values, leaders can help staff develop and support a changing vision. Leaders also must carefully listen to the group to be sure that the group moves forward and does not disengage as changes are implemented. That is, leaders need to go fast enough to keep the organization moving, but slow enough to engage most of the people in the changes. Achieving this delicate balance between change and stability is a major challenge for most leaders.

In visualizing the ideal, leaders should pay attention to their own emotions and connect emotions to vision. Facts alone will not cause people to change and to adopt a new culture. Rather people will adapt when they are both intellectually and emotionally engaged in the change process.

As an ideal vision is developed and the group begins to embrace the change, the leader develops systems to sustain emotionally intelligent practices.[26] Core competencies that emphasize emotionally intelligent behaviors, positive attitudes, and engaged employees will signal to employees that behaviors that support the organization will be rewarded. Rules and regulations that support positive group interactions will align with the desired outcomes, providing staff with a consistent message of how the organization will function. When organizational systems support the desired culture, leaders will have the foundation and tools they need to remove or decrease the influence of toxic employees.

On a more practical level, Willie Petersen, in *Reinventing Strategy,* provides leaders with succinct advice on how to lead a change effort. His six steps include:

1. create a compelling statement for change
2. communicate honestly and constantly

3. maximize participation

4. remove those who won't change

5. generate short-term wins

6. set a shining example[27]

Petersen's steps mesh well with the advice from Buckingham and Coffman, as well as Goleman, on changing the organization. Creating a compelling statement for change begins the process of emotionally engaging employees in the change. The case for change explains to staff why the change is important and what will happen. It answers staff needs for information, for understanding, and helps employees begin to understand how they can contribute to the change.

Effective communication is accomplished when leaders are authentic and exhibit integrity and honesty. Employees will pick up on signals that indicate the leader is not telling the truth, is not authentic, and is hiding emotions. Staff will disengage from the process when they sense dissonance and distrust.

Maximizing participation is always a key part of a change process and a process of reinventing organizational culture. Employees are more apt to accept changes when they are a part of the implementation process. Employees who feel valued by the organization, who see a role for themselves within the organization, are more likely to support a change in culture and to work to ensure success.

Removing or marginalizing resisters or toxic employees is not a pleasant task for leaders. However, as noted throughout the work on emotional intelligence, toxic employees influence others and can create a negative environment and unsuccessful unit even when others in the unit are usually good employees. Too often managers and leaders have underestimated the impact of negative emotions on a unit. Removing a negative employee from a unit can benefit all the others in the unit. The change occurs quickly. Once negative forces are removed in the workplace, optimistic and hopeful behaviors can flourish.

Generating short-term wins helps people see progress and gain encouragement that the change in the organization will be successful. Celebrating small success is a positive way to keep people engaged in a long process, and taps into their emotional needs for recognition and positive reinforcement.

Finally, leaders must set a positive example demonstrating the behaviors that are part of the change and part of the new culture. Changing cultures is a long process. Leaders need to find the strength to generate optimism and positive emotions throughout the process, acknowledging setbacks while instilling the idea that success is achievable.

In looking at the connection between emotional intelligence and organizational change and culture, it is clear that "emotionally intelligent leaders . . . use resonance-building leadership styles and create norms that foster healthy effective working relationships."[28] These leaders do not breed fear. Instead they build on the organizational vision and mission to engage employees in the organization so that the group will connect emotionally with the organization in a positive way, giving them an understanding of how meaningful their work is to the organization.

CONCLUSION

The changing landscape in which academic libraries function makes effective leadership all the more necessary to achieve a positive future that addresses the concerns of Campbell and others, namely, ensuring that academic libraries remain in existence and, more importantly, play a dynamic role in helping their institutions meet their stated mission and in working toward the accomplishment of the institutional vision. In that future, libraries compete effectively for resources, become effective players in achieving the various roles that Neal identifies, and assume an integral role in a learning and research culture. Leaders cannot be ignorant of leadership theories, such as emotional intelligence, and their application to the workplace and organizational effectiveness. Nonetheless, leadership extends beyond an institutional or library setting and involves interaction with more stakeholders and players having competing interests.

A good example is information policy, a field encompassing both public policy and information science, which treats information as both a commodity—adheres to the economic theory of property rights—and a resource to be collected, protected, shared, manipulated, managed, and retained. Information policy then is a set of interrelated principles, laws, guidelines, rules, regulations, and procedures guiding the oversight and management of the information *life cycle:* the collection, production, distribution and dissemination, retrieval and use, retirement, and preservation of information. Information policy also embraces access to, and use of, information and records; records relate to the conduct of government or institutional business and provide an audit trail for holding governments and institutions accountable. Collectively, policies form a framework that "profoundly affects the manner in which an individual in a society, indeed a society itself, makes political, economic, and social choices."[29]

Academic and other library leaders must be able to participate in discussions and the shaping of information policies at the local, state, national, and international levels. In so doing, they will have to seek support among competing interests and policy makers, and be able to engage in compromise that advances the library position on issues related to access to information and records, intellectual property rights, privacy, scholarly communication, and more.

Current and future leaders must continue to develop their abilities, knowledge, and skills if they are to suceed in changing the environment. They should also view mentoring as an obligation, treating mentoring as a learning process for both those mentored and themselves to develop future leaders with the knowledge and skills to ensure success.

"By and large, the libraries many professionals prepared themselves to work in and lead do not exist any more. (Practitioners who graduated less than six months ago might be an exception to this broad generalization.)"[30]

NOTES

1. Jerry D. Campbell, "Changing a Cultural Icon: The Academic Library as a Virtual Destination," *EDUCAUSE Review* 41 (January/February 2006): 30.

2. Peggy L. Maki and Nancy A. Borkowski, eds., *The Assessment of Doctoral Education: Emerging Criteria and New Methods for Improving Outcomes* (Sterling, VA: Stylus Publishing, 2006), 3.

3. Campbell, "Changing a Cultural Icon," 16.

4. Ibid., 30.

5. See, for instance, Elizabeth J. Wood, Rush Miller, and Amy Knapp, *Beyond Survival: Managing Academic Libraries in Transition* (Westport, CT: Libraries Unlimited, 2007), chap. 1; Peter Hernon and Nancy Rossiter, *Making a Difference: Leadership and Academic Libraries* (Westport, CT: Libraries Unlimited, 2007), chaps. 1, 17, and 18.

6. See Gregg Sapp and Ron Gilmour, "A Brief History of the Future of Academic Libraries: Predictions and Speculations from the Literature of the Profession, 1975 to 2000. Part One, 1975 to 1989," *portal: Libraries and the Academy* 2, no. 4 (2002): 553–76; Gregg Sapp and Ron Gilmour, "A Brief History of the Future of Academic Libraries: Predictions and Speculations from the Literature of the Profession, 1975 to 2000. Part Two, 1990 to 2000," *portal: Libraries and the Academy* 3, no. 1 (2003): 13–34.

7. Philip J. Goldstein, "The Future of Higher Education: A View from CHEMA," The Council of Higher Education Management Associates, http://www.ala.org/ala/acrl/acrlissues/futureofacademiclibrariesandhighereducation/APPA39a_ScreenOpt.pdf (accessed January 28, 2007).

8. Ibid., 16.

9. W. Lee Hisle, "Top Issues Facing Academic Libraries: A Report of the Focus on the Future Task Force," *College & Research Libraries News* 63, no. 10 (November 2002): 714–15, 730.

10. James G. Neal, "You Can't Rollerskate in a Buffalo Herd: Leading and Managing in a Political Context," unpublished presentation delivered at the Simmons College program in managerial leadership in the information professions, Seattle, WA, January 23, 2007.

11. James G. Neal, "The Entrepreneurial Imperative: Advancing from Incremental to Radical Change in the Academic Library," *portal: Libraries and the Academy* 1, no. 1 (2001): 1–13.

12. Ibid., 2.

13. Ibid., 12.

14. Wood, Miller, and Knapp, *Beyond Survival*, 93–94. See also G. Edward Evans and Patricia Layzell Ward, *Leadership Basics for Librarians and Information Professionals* (Lanham, MD: Scarecrow Press, 2007).

15. See Wayne A. Wiegand, ed., *Leaders in American Academic Librarianship, 1925–1975* (Pittsburgh, PA: Beta Phi Mu, 1983).

16. "100 of the Most Important Leaders We Had in the 20th Century (Library Leaders)," *American Libraries*, 30, no. 11 (December 1999): 38–46.

17. National Institute of Standards and Technology, *Education Criteria for Performance Excellence* (Gaithersburg, MD: National Institute of Standards and Technology, 2006), http://baldrige.nist.gov/Education_Criteria.htm (accessed January 13, 2007).

18. See Hernon and Rossiter, *Making a Difference*, chap. 15.

19. Richard Boyatzis and Anne McKee, *Resonant Leadership* (Boston: Harvard Business School Press, 2005), 44.

20. Gary R. Howard, "Whites in Multicultural Education: Rethinking Our Role," *Phi Delta Kappa* 75, no. 1 (September 1993): 39.

21. Tamara Woodbury, "Building Organizational Culture Word by Word," *Leader to Leader* no. 39 (Winter 2006): 48–54.

22. Marcus Buckingham and Curt Coffman, *First, Break All the Rules* (New York: Simon and Schuster, 1999): 42–49.

23. Joan Giesecke, *Fundamentals of Library Supervision* (Chicago: American Library Association, 2005), 37.

24. Daniel Goleman, Richard Boyatzis, and Annie McKee, *Primal Leadership: Realizing the Power of Emotional Intelligence* (Boston, MA: Harvard Business School Press, 2002), 21.

25. Ibid., 218.

26. Ibid., 222.

27. Willie Petersen, *Reinventing Strategy: Using Strategic Learning to Create and Sustain Breakthrough Performance* (New York: Wiley & Sons, 2002), 197–98.

28. Goleman, Boyatzis, and McKee, *Primal Leadership*, 223.

29. Marilyn Gell Mason, *The Federal Role in Library and Information Services* (White Plains, NY: Knowledge Industry Publications, 1983), 93.

30. Wood, Miller, and Knapp, *Beyond Survival*, 190.

BIBLIOGRAPHY

ARTICLES

Alire, Camila A. "Diversity and Leadership: The Color of Leadership." *Journal of Library Administration* 32, no. 3/4 (2001): 95–109.

Alon, Ilan, and James M. Higgins. "Global Leadership Success through Emotional and Cultural Intelligences." *Business Horizons* 48 (2005): 501–12.

Ancona, Deborah, Thomas W. Malone, Wanda J. Orlikowski, and Peter M. Senge. "In Praise of the Incomplete Leader." *Harvard Business Review* 85, no. 2 (February 2007): 92–100.

Antonakis, John. "Why 'Emotional Intelligence' Does not Predict Leadership Effectiveness: A Comment on Prati, Douglas, Ferris, Ammeter, and Buckley (2003)." *The International Journal of Organizational Analysis* 11, no. 4 (2003): 355–61.

Ashkanasy, Neal M., and Catherine S. Daus. "Emotion in the Workplace: The New Challenge for Managers." *Academy of Management Executive* 16 (2002): 76–86.

Ashkanasy, Neal M., and Catherine S. Daus. "Rumors of the Death of Emotional Intelligence in Organizational Behavior Are Vastly Exaggerated." *Journal of Organizational Behavior* 26 (2005): 441–52.

Bossidy, Larry. "What Your Leader Expects of You and What You Should Expect in Return." *Harvard Business Review* 85, no. 3 (April 2007): 58–65.

Boyatzis, Richard E., and Annie McKee. "Intentional Change." *Journal of Organizational Excellence* 25, no. 3 (2006): 49.

Brown, F. William, and Dan Moshavi. "Transformational Leadership and Emotional Intelligence: A Potential Pathway for an Increased Understanding of Interpersonal Influence." *Journal of Organizational Behavior* 26, no. 7 (November 2005): 867–71.

Brown, F. William, Scott E. Bryant, and Michael D. Reilly. "Does Emotional Intelligence—as Measured by the EQI—Influence Transformational Leadership and/or Desirable Outcomes?" *Leadership & Organization Development Journal* 27, no. 5 (2006): 330–51.

Bryman, Alan. "Qualitative Research on Leadership: A Critical but Appreciative Review." *Leadership Quarterly* 15, no. 6 (2004): 729–69.

Campbell, Jerry D. "Changing a Cultural Icon: The Academic Library as a Virtual Destination." *EDUCAUSE Review* 41 (January/February 2006): 16–30.

Chen, Chao C., and James R. Meindl. "The Construction of Leadership Images in the Popular Press: The Case of Donald Burr and People Express." *Administrative Science Quarterly* 36, no. 4 (1991): 521–51.

Cherniss, Cary, Melissa Extein, Daniel Goleman, and Roger P. Weissberg. "Emotional Intelligence: What Does the Research Really Indicate." *Educational Psychologist* 41, no. 4 (Fall 2006): 239–46.

Conger, Jay A. "Qualitative Research as the Cornerstone Methodology for Understanding Leadership." *Leadership Quarterly* 9, no. 1 (1998): 107–21.

Conte, Jeffrey M. "A Review and Critique of Emotional Intelligence Measures." *Journal of Organizational Behavior* 26, no. 4 (2005): 433–40.

Cooper, Robert K. "Applying Emotional Intelligence in the Workplace." *Training & Development* 51, no. 12 (December 1997): 31–38.

Cummings, Greta, Leslie Hayduk, and Carole Estabrooks. "Mitigating the Impact of Hospital Restructuring on Nurses: The Responsibility of Emotionally Intelligent Leadership." *Nursing Research* 54, no. 1 (January/February 2005): 9–11.

Dasborough, Marie T. "Cognitive Asymmetry in Employee Emotional Reactions to Leadership Behaviors." *The Leadership Quarterly* 17 (2006): 163–78.

Downey, L. A., V. Papageorgiou, and C. Stough. "Examining the Relationship between Leadership, Emotional Intelligence, and Intuition in Senior Female Managers." *Leadership & Organization Development Journal* 27, no. 4 (2006): 250–64.

Dulewicz, Victor, and Malcolm Higgs. "Emotional Intelligence: A Review and Evaluation Study." *Journal of Managerial Psychology* 15, no. 4 (2000): 341–72.

Ford, David L. Jr., and Kiran M. Ismail. "Perceptions of Effective Leadership among Central Eurasian Managers: A Cultural Convergence-divergence Examination within a Globalization Context." *Journal of International Management* 12, no. 2 (2006): 158–80.

Fry, Louis W. "Toward a Theory of Spiritual Leadership." *The Leadership Quarterly* 14, no. 6 (2003): 693–728.

Gardner, Howard, and Thomas Hatch. "Multiple Intelligences Go to School: Educational Implications of the Theory of Multiple Intelligences." *Educational Researcher* 18, no. 8 1989): 4–9.

George, Bill, Peter Sims, Andrew N. McLean, and Diana Mayer. "Discovering Your Authentic Leadership." *Harvard Business Review* 85, no. 2 (February 2007): 129–38.

George, Jennifer M. "Emotions and Leadership: The Role of Emotional Intelligence." *Human Relations* 53, no. 8 (2000): 1027–1044.

Giesecke, Joan, and Beth McNeil. "Transitioning to the Learning Organization." *Library Trends* 53, no. 1 (Summer 2004): 54–67.

Goleman, Daniel. "What Makes a Leader?" *Harvard Business Review* 76, no. 6 (November/December 1998): 93–102; *Harvard Business Review* 82, no. 1 (January 2004): 82–91.

Gronn, Peter C., and Peter Ribbins. "Leaders in Context: Postpositivist Approaches to Understanding Educational Leadership." *Educational Administration Quarterly* 32 (1996): 452.

Groves, Kevin S. "Integrating Leadership Development and Succession Planning Best Practices." *Journal of Management Development* 26, no. 3 (2007): 239–60.

Hernon, Peter, and Nancy Rossiter. "Emotional Intelligence: Which Traits Are Most Prized?" *College & Research Libraries* 67, no. 3 (May 2006): 260–75.

Hernon, Peter, Ronald R. Powell, and Arthur P. Young. "Academic Library Directors: What Do They Do?" *College & Research Libraries* 65, no. 6 (Nov. 2004): 539–40.

Hewlett, Sylvia Ann, and Carolyn Buck Luce. "Extreme Jobs: The Dangerous Allure of the 70-hour Workweek." *Harvard Business Review* 84, no. 12 (December 2006): 49–59.

Hewlett, Sylvia Ann, Carolyn Buck Luce, and Cornel West. "Leadership in Your Midst: Tapping the Hidden Strengths of Minority Executives." *Harvard Business Review* 83, no. 11 (November, 2005): 74–82.

Higgs, Malcolm. "Do Leaders Need Emotional Intelligence? A Study of the Relationship between Emotional Intelligence and Leadership of Change." *International Journal of Organisational Behaviour* 5, no. 6 (2002): 195–212.

Higgs, Malcolm. "How Can We Make Sense of Leadership in the 21st Century?" *Leadership & Organization Development Journal* 24, no. 5 (2002): 273–84.

Higgs, Malcolm. "Is There a Relationship between the Myers-Briggs Type Indicator and Emotional Intelligence?" *Journal of Managerial Psychology* 16, no. 7 (2001): 509–33.

Hisle, W. Lee. "Top Issues Facing Academic Libraries: A Report of the Focus on the Future Task Force." *College & Research Libraries News* 63, no. 10 (November 2002): 714–15, 730.

Howard, Gary R. "Whites in Multicultural Education: Rethinking Our Role." *Phi Delta Kappa* 75, no. 1 (September 1993): 36–41.

Kellett, Janet B., Ronald H. Humphrey, ands Randall G. Sleeth. "Empathy and the Emergence of Task and Relations Leaders." *The Leadership Quarterly* 17 (2006): 146–62.

Kerr, Robert, John Garvin, Norma Heaton, and Emily Boyle. "Emotional Intelligence and Leadership Effectiveness." *Leadership & Organization Development Journal* 27, no. 4 (April 2006): 265–79.

Korukonda, Appa Rao, and James G. Hunt. "Premisses and Paradigms in Leadership Research." *Journal of Organizational Change Management* 4, no. 2 (1991): 19–33.

Kupers, Wendelin, and Jürgen Weibler. "How Emotional Is Transformational Leadership Really?" *Leadership & Organization Development Journal* 27, no. 5 (2006): 368–83.

Lakshman, C. "Organizational Knowledge Leadership: A Grounded Theory Approach." *Leadership & Organization Development Journal* 28, no. 1 (2007): 51–75.

Langley, Andrew. "Emotional Intelligence: A New Evaluation for Management Development?" *Career Development International* 5, no. 3 (2000): 177–83.

Law, Kenneth S. Chi-Sum Wong, and Lynda L. Song. "The Construct and Criterion Validity of Emotional Intelligence and Its Potential Utility for Management Studies." *Journal of Applied Psychology* 89, no. 3 (2004): 483–96.

Madsen, Susan R. "Developing Leadership: Exploring Childhoods of Women University Presidents." *Journal of Educational Administration* 45, no. 1 (2007): 99–118.

Mandell, Barbara, and Shilpa Pherwani. "Relationship between Emotional Intelligence and Transformational Leadership Style: A Gender Comparison." *Journal of Business & Psychology* 17, no. 3 (2003): 387–402.

Mayer, John D., and Peter Salovey. "The Intelligence of Emotional Intelligence." *Intelligence* 17 (1993): 433–42.

Mayer, John D., Peter Salovey, D. R. Caruso, and G. Sitarenios. "Emotional Intelligence as a Standard Intelligence." *Emotion* 1 (2001): 232–42.

McCauley, Cynthia D., Wilfred H. Drath, Charles J. Palus, Patricia M. G. O'Connor, and Becca A. Baker. "The Use of Constructive-Development Theory to Advance the Understanding of Leadership." *The Leadership Quarterly* 17 (2006): 634–53.

McKee, Annie, and Richard E. Boyatzis. "Inspiring Others through Resonant Leadership." *Business Strategy Review* 17, no. 2 (2006): 17.

McKee, Annie, and Richard E. Boyatzis. "Renewing and Sustaining Leadership." *Leader to Leader* 40 (2006): 30–31.

McKee, Annie, and Dick Massimilian. "Resonant Leadership: A New Kind of Leadership for the Digital Age." *Journal of Business Strategy* 27, no. 5 (2006): 45–49.

McKee, Annie, Frances Johnston, and Richard Massimilian. "Mindfulness, Hope, and Compassion: A Leader's Road Map to Renewal." *Ivey Business Journal* 70, no. 5 (May/June 2006): 1–5.

Moss, Simon, Damian Ritossa, and Simon Ngu. "The Effect of Follower Regulatory Focus and Extroversion of Leadership Behavior: The Role of Emotional Intelligence." *Journal of Individual Differences* 27, no. 2 (June 2006): 93–107.

Neal, James G. "The Entrepreneurial Imperative: Advancing from Incremental to Radical Change in the Academic Library." *portal: Libraries and the Academy* 1, no. 1 (2001): 1–13.

"100 of the Most Important Leaders We Had in the 20th Century (Library Leaders)." *American Libraries,* 30, no. 11 (December 1999): 38–46.

Paek, Ellen. "Religiosity and Perceived Emotional Intelligence among Christians." *Personality and Individual Differences* 41 (2006): 479–90.

Palmer, Benjamin R., Gilles Gignac, Ramesh Manocha, and Con Stough. "A Psychometric Evaluation of the Mayer-Salovey-Caruso Emotional Intelligence Test Version 2.0." *Intelligence* 33 (2005): 285–305.

Pauchant, Thierry C. "Integral Leadership: A Research Proposal." *Journal of Organizational Change Management* 18, no. 2 (2005): 211–29.

Petrides, K. V., and Adrian Furham. "On the Dimensional Structure of Emotional Intelligence." *Personality and Individual Differences* 29, no. 2 (August 2000): 313–20.

Prati, L. Melita, Ceasar Douglas, Gerald R. Ferris, Anthony P. Ammeter, and M. Ronald Buckley. "Emotional Intelligence Leadership Effectiveness, and

Team Outcomes." *The International Journal of Organizational Analysis* 11, no. 1 (2003): 21–40.

Raffel, Dawn. "The Two Self-Defeating Habits of Otherwise Brilliant People." *O, the Oprah Magazine* 7, no. 9 (September 2006): 295–6.

Roberts, Richard D., Ralf Schulze, Kristin O'Brien, Carolyn MacCann, John Reid, and Andy Maul. "Exploring the Validity of the Mayer-Salovey-Caruso Emotional Intelligence Test (MSCEIT) with Established Emotions Measures." *Emotion* 6, no. 4 (November 2006): 663–69.

Rubin, Robert S., David C. Munz, and William H. Bommer. "Leading from Within: The Effects of Emotion Recognition and Personality on Transformational Leadership Behavior." *Academy of Management Journal* 48, no. 5 (2005): 845–58.

Salovey, Peter, and John D. Mayer. "Emotional Intelligence." *Imagination, Cognition, and Personality* 9 (1990): 185–211.

Sapp, Gregg, and Ron Gilmour. "A Brief History of the Future of Academic Libraries: Predictions and Speculations from the Literature of the Profession, 1975 to 2000. Part One, 1975 to 1989." *portal: Libraries and the Academy* 2, no. 4 (2002): 553–76.

Sapp, Gregg, and Ron Gilmour. "A Brief History of the Future of Academic Libraries: Predictions and Speculations from the Literature of the Profession, 1975 to 2000. Part Two, 1990 to 2000." *portal: Libraries and the Academy* 3, no. 1 (2003): 13–34

Sosik, John J., and Lara E. Megerian. "Understanding Leader Emotional Intelligence and Performance: The Role of Self-other Agreement on Transformational Leadership Perceptions." *Group & Organization Management* 24, no. 3 (September 1999): 367–90.

Sy, Thomas, Susanna Tram, and Linda A. O'Hara. "Relation of Employee and Managerial Emotional Intelligence to Job Satisfaction and Performance." *Journal of Vocational Behavior* 68 (2006): 461–73.

Warner, Linda Sue, and Keith Grint, "American Indian Ways of Leading and Knowing." *Leadership* 2, no. 2 (May 2006): 225–244.

Waterhouse, Lynn. "Multiple Intelligences, the Mozart Effect, and Emotional Intelligence: A Critical Review." *Educational Psychologist* 41, no. 4 (Fall 2006): 216–218.

Whittington, J. Lee, Tricia M. Pitts, Woody V. Kagler, and Vicki L. Goodwin. "Legacy Leadership: The Leadership Wisdom of the Apostle Paul." *The Leadership Quarterly* 16 (2005): 749–70.

Wolf, Steven B., Anthony T. Pescosolido, and Vanessa U. Druskat. "Emotional Intelligence as the Basis of Leadership Emergence in Self-managing Teams." *Leadership Quarterly* 13, no. 5 (2002): 505–22.

Wong, Chi-Sum, and Kenneth S. Law. "The Effect of Leader and Follower Emotional Intelligence on Performance and Attitude: An Exploratory Study." *The Leadership Quarterly* 13, no. 3 (June 2002): 243–274.

Wood, James A., and Bruce E. Winston. "Development of Three Scales to Measure Leader Accountability." *Leadership & Organization Development Journal* 28, no. 2 (2007): 167–85.

Woodbury, Tamara. "Building Organizational Culture Word by Word." *Leader to Leader* no. 39 (Winter, 2006): 48–54.

Zeidner, Moshe, Gerald Matthews, and Richard D. Roberts. "Emotional Intelligence in the Workplace: A Critical Review." *Applied Psychology: An International Review* 53, no. 3 (2004): 371–99.

BOOKS

Albrecht, Karl. *Social Intelligence: The New Science of Success.* San Francisco: Jossey-Bass, 2006.

Axelrod, Alan. *Elizabeth I, CEO: Strategic Lessons from the Leader Who Built an Empire.* New York: Prentice Hall Books, 2000.

Bar-On, Reuven. *Bar-On Emotional Quotient Inventory: Technical Manual.* Toronto: Multi Health Systems, 1997.

Bass, Bernard M., and Ronald E. Riggio. *Transformational Leadership.* 2nd ed. Mahwah, NJ: Lawrence Erlbaum Associates, 2006.

Bennis, Warren. *On Becoming a Leader.* Reading, MA: Addison-Wesley, 1989.

Blake, Robert R., and Jane S. Mouton. *The Managerial Grid: Key Orientations for Achieving Production through People.* Houston, TX: Gulf, 1964.

Blake, Robert R., and Jane S. Mouton. *The New Managerial Grid.* Houston, TX: Gulf, 1978.

Blake, Robert R., and Jane S. Mouton. *The Managerial Grid III.* Houston, TX: Gulf, 1985.

Bolman, Lee, and Terrence Deal. *Reframing Organizations.* San Francisco: Jossey-Bass Publishers, 1991.

Bolton, Sharon C. *Emotion Management in the Workplace.* New York: Palgrave Macmillan, 2005.

Boyatzis, Richard, and Annie McKee. *Resonant Leadership: Renewing Yourself and Connecting with Others through Mindfulness, Hope, and Compassion.* Boston: Harvard Business School Press, 2005.

Buckingham, Marcus, and Curt Coffman. *First, Break All the Rules.* New York: Simon and Schuster, 1999.

Druskat, Vanessa Urch, Fabio Sala, and Gerald Mount, eds. *Linking Emotional Intelligence and Performance at Work: Current Research Evidence with Individuals and Groups* (Mahwah, NJ: Lawrence Erlbaum Associates, 2006).

Evans, G. Edward, and Patricia Layzell Ward. *Leadership Basics for Librarians and Information Professionals.* Lanham, MD: Scarecrow Press, 2007.

Gardner, Howard. *Multiple Intelligence: The Theory in Practice.* New York: Basic Books, 1993.

Giesecke, Joan. *Fundamentals of Library Supervision.* Chicago: American Library Association, 2005.

Giesecke Joan, ed. *Scenario Planning for Libraries.* Chicago: American Library Association, 1998.

Goleman, Daniel. *Emotional Intelligence.* New York: Bantam Books, 1995.

Goleman, Daniel. *Social Intelligence: The New Science of Human Relationships.* New York: Bantam, 2006.

Goleman, Daniel. *Working with Emotional Intelligence.* New York: Bantam Books, 1998.

Goleman, Daniel, Richard Boyatzis, and Annie McKee. *Primal Leadership: Realizing the Power of Emotional Intelligence.* Boston, MA: Harvard Business School Press, 2002.

Hernon, Peter, and Nancy Rossiter, eds. *Making a Difference: Leadership and Academic Libraries.* Westport, CT: Libraries Unlimited, 2007.

Hernon, Peter, Ronald R. Powell, and Arthur P. Young. *The Next Library Leadership: Attributes of Academic and Public Library Directors.* Westport, CT: Libraries Unlimited, 2003.

Kouzes, James M., and Barry Z. Posner. *Credibility: How Leaders Gain and Lose It, and Why People Demand It.* San Francisco: Jossey-Bass, 1993.

Kouzes, James M., and Barry Z. Posner. *Encouraging the Heart: A Leader's Guide to Rewarding and Recognizing Others.* San Francisco: Jossey-Bass, 1999.

Lynn, Adele B. *The EQ Difference: A Powerful Plan for Putting Emotional Intelligence to Work.* New York: AMACOM, 2005.

Maki, Peggy L., and Nancy A. Borkowski, eds. *The Assessment of Doctoral Education: Emerging Criteria and New Methods for Improving Outcomes.* Sterling, VA: Stylus Publishing, 2006.

Mason, Marilyn Gell. *The Federal Role in Library and Information Services.* White Plains, NY: Knowledge Industry Publications, 1983.

Matthews, Gerald, Moshe Zeidner, and Richard D. Roberts. *Emotional Intelligence: Science and Myth.* Cambridge, MA: The MIT Press, 2002.

McGregor, Douglas. *Human Side of Enterprise.* New York: McGraw-Hill, 1960.

Northouse, Peter. *Leadership, Theory, and Practice.* Thousand Oaks, CA: Sage Publications, 2004.

Petersen, Willie. *Reinventing Strategy: Using Strategic Learning to Create and Sustain Breakthrough Performance.* New York: Wiley & Sons, 2002.

Powell, Ronald R., and Lynn Silipigni Connaway. *Basic Research Methods for Librarians.* 4th ed. Westport, CT: Libraries Unlimited, 2004.

Riggio, Ronald E., Susan E. Murphy, and Francis J. Pirozzolo. *Multiple Intelligences and Leadership.* Mahwah, NJ: Lawrence Erlbaum Associates, 2002.

Robson, Colin. *Real World Research: A Resource for Social Scientists and Practitioner-Researchers.* Oxford, UK: Blackwell, 1993.

Senge, Peter. *The Fifth Discipline: The Art and Practice of the Learning Organization.* New York: Doubleday, 1990.

Steiner, Claude. *Achieving Emotional Literacy.* New York: Avon Books, 1997.

Taylor, Steven, and Robert Bogdan. *Introduction to Qualitative Research Methods.* 2nd ed. New York: Wiley and Sons, 1984.

Weisinger, Hendrie. *Emotional Intelligence at Work: The Untapped Edge for Success.* San Francisco: Jossey-Bass Publishers, 1998.

Wiegand, Wayne A., ed. *Leaders in American Academic Librarianship, 1925–1975.* Pittsburgh, PA: Beta Phi Mu, 1983.

Wood, Elizabeth J., Rush Miller, and Amy Knapp. *Beyond Survival: Managing Academic Libraries in Transition.* Westport, CT: Libraries Unlimited, 2007.

BOOK CHAPTERS

Goleman, Daniel. "An EI-based Theory of Performance." In *The Emotionally Intelligent Workplace: How to Select for, Measure, and Improve Emotional Intelligence in Individuals, Groups, and Organizations.* Edited by Cary Cherniss and David Goleman. San Francisco, CA: Jossey-Bass, 2001.

Mayer, John D., and Peter Salovey. "What Is Emotional Intelligence." In *Emotional Development and Emotional Intelligence: Educational Implications*. Edited by Peter Salovey and David J. Sluyter. New York: Basic Books, 1997.

DISSERTATIONS AND THESES

Bryson, Karen D. Lokelani. *Managerial Success and Derailment: The Relationship between Emotional Intelligence and Leadership*. Doctoral diss., East Tennessee State University, 2005. Available from *Dissertations & Theses: Full Text*, AAT 315997.

Buontempo, Gina. *Emotional Intelligence and Decision Making: The Impact of Judgment Biases*. Doctoral diss., Columbia University, 2005. Available from *Dissertations & Theses: Full Text*, AAT 3174752.

Burbach, Mark E. *Testing the Relationship between Emotional Intelligence and Full-range Leadership as Moderated by Cognitive Style and Self-concept*. Doctoral diss., University of Nebraska, Lincoln, 2004. Available from *Dissertations & Theses: Full Text*, AAT 31269944.

Campbell, Mary K. *Exploring the Relationship between Emotional Intelligence, Intuition, and Responsible Risk-taking in Organizations*. Doctoral diss., California School of Professional Psychology, 2000. Available from *Dissertations & Theses: Full Text*, AAT 9997529.

Collins, Virginia L. *Emotional Intelligence and Leadership Success*. Doctoral diss., University of Nebraska, Lincoln, 2001. Available from *Dissertations & Theses: Full Text*, AAT 3034371.

Cook, Charles R. *Effects of Emotional Intelligence on Principals' Leadership Performance*. Doctoral diss., Montana State University, Bozeman, 2006. Available from *Dissertations & Theses: Full Text*, AAT 3206272.

Cummings, Greta G. *An Examination of the Effects of Hospital Restructuring on Nurses: How Emotionally Intelligent Leadership Styles Mitigate These Effects*. Doctoral diss., University of Alberta (Canada), 2003.

Gardner, Mary Frances L. *An Analysis of a Woman Administrator's Leadership Competency Behaviors*. Doctoral diss., University of Arkansas, 2004. Available from *Dissertations & Theses: Full Text*, AAT 3158061.

Gerrish, Sheila Rogers. *A Study of the Relationship of Principal Emotional Intelligence Competencies to Middle School Organizational Climate and Health in the State of Washington*. Doctoral diss., Seattle Pacific University, 2005. Available from *Dissertations & Theses: Full Text*, AAT 3178673.

Johnson, Lisa. *An Analysis of Major Facilitators to Their Success as Reported by Successful Women Administrators*. Doctoral diss., East Tennessee State University, 2005. Available from *Dissertations & Theses: Full Text*, AAT 3195376.

Macrae, Judith. *Self-awareness: The Missing Link to Leadership?* Doctoral diss., Royal Roads University (Canada), 2004. Available from *Dissertations & Theses: Full Text*, AAT MQ93750.

Payne, Wayne L. *A Study of Emotion: Developing Emotional Intelligence, Self-integration, Relating to Fear, Pain and Desire (Theory, Structure of Reality, Problem-solving, Contraction/expansion, Tuning in/comingout/letting Go)*. Doctoral diss., The Union for Experimenting Colleges and Universities [now The Union Institute], 1985. Available from *Dissertations & Theses: Full Text*, AAT 8605928.

Schulte, Melanie J. *Emotional Intelligence: A Predictive or Descriptive Construct in Ascertaining Leadership Style or a New Name for Old Knowledge?* Doctoral diss., Our Lady of the Lake University, 2003. Available from *Dissertations & Theses: Full Text,* AAT 33068435.

Smith, Renée M. *An Examination of the Relationship between Emotional Intelligence and Leader Effectiveness.* Doctoral diss., Nova Southeastern University, 2006. Available from *Dissertations & Theses: Full Text,* AAT 3205547.

Weinberger, Lisa A. *An Examination of the Relationship between Emotional Intelligence, Leadership Style and Perceived Leadership Effectiveness.* Doctoral diss., University of Minnesota, 2003. Available from *Dissertations & Theses: Full Text,* AAT 3113218.

Yancey-Bragg, Terry. *Leadership Theories, Perceptions and Assessments: The Relationship of African American Women in a Fortune 500 Company.* Doctoral diss., Wilmington College, 2006. Available from *Dissertations & Theses: Full Text,* AAT 3189966.

Yorke, Kristi. *A Study of Leadership Theory in Practice: Implementing a Social Responsibility Program at McGill Elementary School.* Doctoral diss., Royal Roads University (Canada), 2005.

WEB RESOURCES

Accel-Team. "Human Relations Contributors: David McClelland." http://www.accel-team.com/human_relations/hrels_06_mcclelland.html (accessed December 30, 2006).

American Library Association, Association of College and Research Libraries. "Excellence in Academic Libraries Award." Association of College and Research Libraries, 2007. http://www.ala.org/ala/acrl/acrlawards/excellenceacademic.htm (accessed March 22, 2007).

Answers.com. "Emotional Intelligence Tests." http://www.answers.com/topic/emotional-intelligence-tests (accessed December 8, 2006).

Arminio, Jan L., Sandra Catier, Steven E. Jones, Kevin Kruger, Nance Lucas, Jamie Washington, Nancy Young, and Angela Scoti. "Leadership Experiences Students of Color." *NASPA Journal* 37, no. 3 (Spring 2000): 506. http://publications.naspa.org/cgi/viewcontent.cgi?article = 1112&context = naspajournal (accessed May 22, 2007).

ASE. *The Emotional Intelligence Questionnaire: Managerial & Managerial 360.* http://www.ase-solutions.co.uk/product.asp?id = 22 (accessed December 30, 2006).

Caruso, David. "Example MSCEIT [Test] Items." http://www.emotionaliq.org/MSCEITExamples.htm (accessed January 4, 2006).

Caruso, David R, "MSCEIT: Mayer-Salovey-Caruso Emotional Intelligence Test Resource Report." Multi-Health Systems Inc, 2004, 2–4. http://www.mhs.com/ROE/MSCEITResource.pdf (accessed January 4, 2007).

The CEO Refresher. "Leading Change." http://www.refresher.com/!leading (accessed February 7, 2007).

Cherniss, Cary. "Emotional Intelligence: What It Is and Why It Matters." Paper presented at the Annual Meeting of the Society for Industrial and Organizational Psychology, New Orleans, LA, April 15, 2000 (The Consortium for Research on Emotional Intelligence in Organizations). http://www.eiconsortium.

org/research/what_is_emotional_intelligence.htm (accessed December 30, 2006).

The Consortium for Research on Emotional Intelligence in Organizations. *Bar-On Emotional Quotient Inventory EQ-i.* http://www.eiconsortium.org/measures/eqi.htm (accessed December 8, 2006).

The Consortium for Research on Emotional Intelligence in Organizations. *Emotional Intelligence Appraisal.* http://www.eiconsortium.org/measures/emotional_intelligence_appraisal.htm (accessed December 28, 2006).

The Consortium for Research on Emotional Intelligence in Organizations. *The Mayer-Salovey-Caruso Emotional Intelligence Test (MSCEIT).* http://www.eiconsortium.org/measures/msceit.htm (accessed December 20, 2006).

Emmerling, Robert J., and Daniel Goleman. "Emotional Intelligence: Issues and Common Misunderstanding." Rutgers University, The Consortium for Research on Emotional Intelligence in Organizations, 2003. http://www.eiconsortium.org/research/EI_Issues_And_Common_Misunderstandings.pdf (accessed December 36, 2006).

The EQ Store. "Assessment: Mayer-Salovey-Caruso Emotional Intelligence Test + Debrief 87." http://www.6seconds.org/xcart/product.php?productid=87 (accessed January 4, 2007).

Goldstein, Philip J. "The Future of Higher Education: A View from CHEMA." The Council of Higher Education Management Associates. http://www.ala.org/ala/acrl/acrlissues/futureofacademiclibrariesandhighereducation/APPA39a_ScreenOpt.pdf (accessed January 28, 2007).

Hardesty, Larry. "Excellence in Academic Libraries: Recognizing It." *Library Issues: Briefings for Faculty and Administrators 27*, no. 4 (March 2007): 1–3. http://0-www.libraryissues.com.library.simmons.edu/ (accessed March 22, 2007).

Hay Group®. *Emotional Competency Inventory (ECI).* http://www.hayresourcesdirect.haygroup.com/Competency/Assessments_Surveys/Emotional_Competency_Inventory/Overview.asp (accessed December 17, 2006).

Mayer, John D. *Emotional Intelligence Information: A Site Dedicated to Communicating Scientific Information about Emotional Intelligence, Including Relevant Aspects of Emotions, Cognition, and Personality.* http://www.unh.edu/emotional_intelligence/ (accessed December 28, 2006).

Mayer, John D. "What Is Emotional Intelligence (EI)? How Does This Model Compare to Other Approaches to Emotional Intelligence?" http://www.unh.edu/emotional_intelligence/index.html (accessed January 4, 2006).

McKee, Annie, Frances Johnston, and Richard Massimilian. "Mindfulness, Hope, and Compassion: A Leader's Road Map to Renewal," *Ivey Business Journal* 70, no. 5 (May/June 2006): 1–5. Available from General BusinessFile ASAP.

Merriam-Webster Online Dictionary (2006–2007). http://mw1.merriam-webster.com/dictionary/mindfulness (accessed May 15, 2007).

National Institute of Standards and Technology. *Education Criteria for Performance Excellence.* Gaithersburg, MD: National Institute of Standards and Technology, 2006. http://baldrige.nist.gov/Education_Criteria.htm (accessed January 13, 2007).

Palmer, Benjamin R., Gilles Gignac, Ramesh Manocha, and Con Stough. "A Psychometric Evaluation of the Mayer-Salovey-Caruso Emotional Intelligence Test Version 2.0." ERIC EJ698156. http://eric.ed.gov/ERICWebPortal/

Home.portal?_nfpb=true&_pageLabel=RecordDetails&ERICExtSearch_Search
Value_0=EJ698156&ERICExtSearch_SearchType_0=eric_accno&objectId =
0900000b8034c781 (accessed December 8, 2006).

Parry, Ken W. "Grounded Theory and Social Process: A New Direction for Leadership Research," *Leadership Quarterly* 9, no. 1 (1998), 21 pages. Available from *Business Source Premier* (accessed March 14, 2007).

Swineburne University. "Emotional Intelligence and Adolescent Classroom Behaviour." http://www.swinburne.edu.au/lss/bsi/eiu/currentei.htm (accessed December 20, 2006).

The Wallace Foundation Education Leadership Action Network. *Educational Leadership Improvement Tool.* http://www.wallacefoundation.org/ELAN/TR/KnowledgeCategories/DevelopingLeaders/PerfMeasurement/ed_ldr_improvement_tool.htm (accessed December 8, 2006).

Wikipedia. "Emotional Intelligence." http://en.wikipedia.org/wiki/Emotional_intelligence (accessed December 6, 2006).

UNPUBLISHED WORK

Kreitz, Patricia. "Leadership and Emotional Intelligence: Study of University Library Directors and Senior Management Teams." Unpublished and in-progress study, PhD program in Managerial Leadership in the Information Professions, Simmons College.

Neal, James G. "You Can't Rollerskate in a Buffalo Herd: Leading and Managing in a Political Context." Presentation delivered at the Simmons College program in managerial leadership in the information professions, Seattle, WA, January 23, 2007.

Wellesley College. Department of Human Resources. Working @Wellesley: An Online Guide to Wellesley College Human Resources. http://www.wellesley.edu/HR/new/VWSite/vwcontents.html (accessed May 7, 2007).

INDEX

ABOUT THE EDITORS
AND CONTRIBUTOR

CAMILA A. ALIRE is Dean Emeritus of University Libraries at the University of New Mexico and is past president of the Association of College and Research Libraries (ACRL). She sits on the Board of Directors of the Association of Research Libraries (ARL) and served on the ALA Executive Board. She served as REFORMA national president and on its Executive Board. She has written on the topic of leadership as well as conducted workshops on leadership development. She received her doctorate in Higher Education Administration from the University of Northern Colorado. She holds an MLS from the University of Denver and a Bachelor of Arts degree from Adams State College.

JOAN GIESECKE is the Dean of Libraries, University of Nebraska-Lincoln (UNL) Libraries. She joined UNL in 1987 and became dean in 1996. Prior to this, she was the Associate Dean for Collections and Services. She has held positions at George Mason University in Fairfax, Virginia, Prince George's County Memorial Library System, and the American Health Care Association. She received a doctorate in public administration from George Mason University, a MLS from the University of Maryland, a master's degree in management from Central Michigan University, and a BA in economics from SUNY at Buffalo. Her research interests include organizational decision making and management skills. She has developed a training program for managers and has presented a variety of papers on management and supervisory skills. She is a former editor of the journal *Library Administration and Management* and has published numerous articles on management issues. Her books include *Practical Help for New Supervisors, Scenario Planning for Libraries,* and *Practical*

Strategies for Library Managers. She is President of the Homestead Girl Scout Council and serves on the Lincoln Rotary Club #14 Board and the Board of the Lincoln Lancaster County United Way.

PETER HERNON is a professor at Simmons College, Graduate School of Library and Information Science, where he teaches courses on government information policy and resources, evaluation of information services, research methods, and academic librarianship. He received his PhD from Indiana University and has taught at Simmons College, the University of Arizona, and Victoria University of Wellington (New Zealand). He is the coeditor of *Library & Information Science Research,* founding editor of *Government Information Quarterly,* and past editor of *The Journal of Academic Librarianship.* He is the author of approximately 275 publications, 45 of which are books. Among these are *Improving the Quality of Library Services for Students with Disabilities, Comparative Perspectives on E-government, Revisiting Outcomes Assessment in Higher Education, Outcomes Assessment in Higher Education,* and *Assessing Service Quality,* which received the Highsmith award for outstanding contribution to the literature of library and information science in 1999.

CHERYL METOYER is associate professor, the Information School, University of Washington, Mary Gates Hall, Box 352840, Suite 370, Seattle, WA 98195–2840: e-mail: metoyer@u.washington.edu. She received her Ph.D. in library and information science from Indiana University. She was also a faculty member at the UCLA Graduate School of Library and Information Studies. From 1993–1997 she held the Rupert Costo Professorship in American Indian History at the University of California, Riverside. In 2006, she was awarded a Rockefeller Fellowship in the Humanities for her research on Native American Systems of Knowledge. Over the years she has served on several advisory boards, including those for the National Commission on Libraries and Information Science, the National Endowment for the Humanities, the National Museum of the American Indian, the U.S. Department of the Interior, the Southwest Museum, the Newberry Library D'Arcy McNickle Center for American Indian History, and the Simmons College's Ph.D. in Managerial Leadership in the Information Professions.